Innovative Selling

Innovative Selling

A Guide to Successful Corporate Professional Selling

Eden White

BEP BUSINESS EXPERT PRESS

Innovative Selling: A Guide to Successful Corporate Professional Selling
Copyright © Business Expert Press, LLC, 2020.

First published in 2020 by
Business Expert Press, LLC
222 East 46th Street, New York, NY 10017
www.businessexpertpress.com

ISBN-13: 978-1-95152-764-8 (paperback)
ISBN-13: 978-1-95152-765-5 (e-book)

Business Expert Press Business Career Development Collection

Collection ISSN: 2642-2123 (print)
Collection ISSN: 2642-2131 (electronic)

Cover image licensed by Ingram Image, StockPhotoSecrets.com
Cover and interior design by S4Carlisle Publishing Services Private Ltd.,
Chennai, India

First edition: 2020

10 9 8 7 6 5 4 3 2 1

Printed in the United States of America.

Media Statements

A unique book for global sales professionals and their sales leaders about how to prepare to manage, cope with, and succeed at corporate global sales.

Recent research has discovered underlying discontent with professional salespeople who represent global sales organizations.

This book assists the sales professionals to navigate the dilemmas and pitfalls that confront today's corporate sellers so they emerge out the other end mentally healthy, skilled, and sane. The book also tackles and simplifies the basic steps of the overall sales process, territory planning, and product training, so as to ultimately improve your sales results.

The content of this book is clear and simple to understand, including many suggestions and recommendations drawn from over 49 years of my own sales knowledge and professional selling experience.

Each chapter is easy to understand so you are able to locate your specific interest quickly. The last two chapters deal with the complexity of real day-to-day selling and the nuts and bolts of the general day to day sales operation.

Many salespeople today are looking for a simple and concise book to guide them through the corporate sales process; I am convinced this is the book.

—Written by a Salesperson for Salespeople.

All professional salespeople and their leaders frequently ask themselves questions they are embarrassed to ask colleagues or their coaches. Finally, here is a book that addresses these difficult situations and answers the questions you are afraid to ask. In addition, this book provides a comprehensive guide to sales planning, customer psychology, and the simple understanding of the seven steps of the sale.

I trust you will enjoy this book and hope it provides answers to many of your burning sales needs.

Our greatest weakness lies in giving up. The most certain way to succeed is always to try just one more time.

—Thomas Edison.

If Thomas Edison was a professional sales person, he would be a great salesperson. Every failed sale has this key element lying within it. Many give up, but the winners always see the possibility of breaking through. Looking from the customer's side, they see determination and a commitment to their business and personal needs.

Abstract

Qualitive Research

My Australian research appears to be similar to that from overseas. Many international salespeople confirm that they experience the same: lack of care and management responsibility. I have been asked many times if my own personal accounts are retaliation against companies I worked for; to this I say absolutely not. The events experienced during my career run true to the research and in no way reflect any animosity toward past employers. I myself was an employer for 13 years and was fortunate to gain insight from both being an employer and being an employee.

At the end of this book, the selling fundamentals are summarized in seven simple steps that are designed to demystify the professional sale process. When you ask professional salespeople to recite the seven steps of the sale, only one in ten can do so. This is concerning. I describe salespeople as running on automatic and not supported within an effective coaching system that works.

I am a strong proponent of a "sales field trainer/coach" accompanying you in the field after completing a basic sales training model. The lack of this core training process is a big problem, and one only hopes companies pick up on this very important training need. Sales managers/leaders need to recognize that part of their position is not only monitoring their team but providing coaching, encouragement, leadership, and direction.

The Australian research clearly pointed to this omission and found room for fundamental improvement along with similar reports in the US and UK.

Finally, your health, happiness, and family are paramount, and the company should take second place when it comes to this important matter. Companies are slowly getting the hint that a healthier sales force is a performing sales force. Promoting your mental health and avoiding stress-related illness are equally important in the overall performance equation.

It is critical to recognize that the welfare of your family is of equal importance to you and that a successful work–life balance is a goal worth striving for.

If a sales person has failed, most companies look at the individual; alternatively, I look to their coach or manager to find out why![1]

Keywords

sales; sales training; sales planning; CRM; sales coaching; professional sales; corporate sales; global sales

---

[1]Eden White Research.

Contents

Preface

Why Is This Book Necessary?

During our sales careers, we take on valuable lessons and, hopefully, alter our behavior putting these lessons into practice so we do not make the same mistakes.

The Science of Selling

Until recently, selling has been considered an art rather than a science. Now it appears to be becoming increasingly recognized as a science. However, there really hasn't been a "science of selling" documented. There has been some science for buyer behavior, but salesperson behavior is too complex to measure. For instance, Pareto's 80/20 rule, applied to studies, have shown that 20 percent of salespeople make 80 percent of the sales revenue, but nobody knows why that 20 percent of salespeople are so much more effective.

Because of the limitations of the tools available to measure selling behavior, it's been impossible to create an actual "science of selling." Despite numerous attempts to redefine selling into a science, it has remained, as it's always been, a poorly understood art in the business world.

My entire working life has been dedicated to professional selling and training within the medical, surgical, and capital domains, spending 49 years devoted to professional sales working for major global companies. This includes 13 years as managing director alongside my wife Robin, company director, for our own medical agency based in Melbourne, Australia.

I held many positions as national and regional sales manager, training manager, and, for many years, sales and marketing manager for South Pacific and Asia Pacific. In addition, I have held various positions in sales training, from international distributorships to direct sales staff within global affiliate operations here and overseas. This includes a 2-year project within a start-up company based in California.

It is fortunate that these companies provided ample management and sales training. I do owe a debt of gratitude to one particular global organization for its dedication to training and its continued commitment to providing regular in-house sales coaching; some of the early sales training methods would not pass basic training methods these days.

Professional selling is a lonely job. Engaging customers on a daily basis is great, but the need for interaction with other salespeople doing the same job can be difficult and can contribute to the development of bad habits.

My 2-year research showed disturbing signs for salespeople's safety, a distinct lack of appropriate product and sales training, and a deficiency in the rudimentary approach and understanding of customer needs. A continuing lack of human resources engagement to resolve conflict within the sales team environment was clear in each feedback research interview.

In the end, salespeople leave their employer, citing job unhappiness, lack of acknowledgment, lies and deception, unresolved conflict, or inadequate remuneration. Not often do salespeople leave companies because they dislike their customers; in fact, the research shows they love dealing with their client base but dislike dealing with the incessant internal politics of their employers. Salespeople dislike and avoid internal politics like the plague and say this is one of the major issues in the modern corporate global sales model today.

I don't wish to demonize global organizations as they provide a huge platform for employment. After working for such juggernauts for many years, it becomes clear you have to accommodate their needs, while they refuse to change and improve their own operations. The system is what it is, and you either toe the line or go elsewhere. The problem with this is that going elsewhere is going down the same path you are already on. The particular industry I sell in has, over the past 15 years, consolidated into a small group of global companies, some of whose global sales exceed the gross domestic product of many small countries.

However, there is light at the end of the tunnel. This book will highlight the selling pitfalls we all face but will include helpful suggestions along the way to make the path to success easier and far less stressful for you and your family. Therefore, I firmly believe we want a job with some degree of security, an employer who really cares about our health and welfare and work–life balance, and a boss who is honest and fights for your rights as a sales team employee.

Enjoy your journey.

Acknowledgments

I dedicate this book to my wife, Robin, and my three children, Cory, Kim, and Joel, for enduring the long weeks when I was absent from home during my international traveling career. Climbing the corporate sales ladder is serious work, and they say "time invested is time reaped." I guess I have spent more time on the road than at home. Thanks to Robin, this book would have never come to fruition.

I would also like to acknowledge several other colleagues I have admired and who have inspired me along the way. Jo Walter, Kylie Jones, Simon Kent, Kim Vega, Sharron Burges, and many others, thank you again for your assistance.

Special thanks should go to my editor, Christine Hoy, for assisting me with such a large undertaking. I am indebted for your help.

I am inspired by and admire these people as they bring to professional sales a sense of natural sales talent, dialogue, and an ability to work at all levels of selling. Finally, a big thank you to Nick Mattiske for his ongoing assistance. In addition, I would like to acknowledge the excellent efforts by Premkumar Narayanan, Project Manager of S4Carlisle Publishing Services and the excellent staff from Business Expert Press for all their incredible help.

Other People I Admire

Many people have I admired in my life, but the following three stand out and have had a big impact on me:

- Professor Stephen Hawking, theoretical physicist (sadly deceased in 2018)
- Neil Degrasse Tyson, astrophysicist
- Professor Brian Cox, particle physicist

Why, you may rightly ask, are scientists my heroes? Simply because these men look to the future and have the tenacity to say how it is. So how does this equate to professional sales? In corporate selling, you need to have a close mentor, look to the future, and have the courage of your convictions. Any hero will do. Just choose one that that you look up to and admire.

My belief is that selling can be encapsulated into three simple concepts:

SEE: To behold and visualize the true opportunity

FEEL: To fully engage the opportunity over the full sales cycle

REALIZE: To fulfill one's potential actualization and crystallize the end goal

These profound three statements are written to foresee the complete opportunity in reality, to fully carry out and engage the customer over the sales cycle, and to completely understand where you are positioned and when the final close will crystallize.

If you can understand the three statements clearly, you have mastered the complete thought process required to be a successful sales person.

How to Use This Book

The content of this book is clear and simple, and many suggestions and recommendations have been provided. Most of these suggestions are my own personal opinions based on my experience, so accept or reject these concepts at your own choice.

You will find "chapter topics" within the contents section so you are able to locate your specific interest directly. Even if you are interested in reading only a particular topic, you would do well to read chapters 1 and 2 first as this will give you a flavor of what the book is about and set the scene for good reading.

The last two chapters deal with the complexity of real day-to-day selling and the nuts and bolts of what is expected in today's professional sales career. Performance is the key, so we deal with many areas that will assist you further to be a winner.

Reference lists are found at the end of the book.

How Will This Book Help You in Sales?

I wish that during my 49-year sales career, there was a book such as this to refer to. Keeping up with modern selling techniques, understanding how to plan effectively, understanding why the boss lies and tells mistruths, down to knowing how to handle a difficult workplace bullying situation or conflict in your sales team are just a few topics I discuss and share throughout this book.

The book aims to help you, the sales professional, understand what lies ahead in your chosen career or, for the more experienced seller, what to do next or how to solve a problem. I have intentionally omitted advice to sales managers and coaches as a future book will deal with these management issues separately.

This book is all about assisting you as a sales professional and shows you how to negotiate the pitfalls along your path and how to use your experience to excel in this dynamic career. It is a wonderful career, and I loved my time in it; however, I trust this book will make the journey a little easier.

CHAPTER 1

Snapshot of Professional Sales Today

Do commercial training courses measure up? You will become more aware of the abundance of sales training courses out there and how to tailor them to meet your needs along with the need for field sales coaching.

Looking at the literature out there provided by the better sales training courses, (RTO, Registered Training Organizations), for example, short in-house sales training courses and the on-line courses; these are well organized. However, all fall short of realistic selling guides and do not include an in-the-field follow-up critique system to guide the seller.

My own coaching–training always included in-the-field coaching, concentrating on planning, customer needs, and customer relationships, and on offering the appropriate product, summarizing, and closing. Many of the in-house courses covered a part of the seven steps of the sale but sadly omitted very important components that salespeople need.

I have not seen any salesperson attend sales training and say, "That was fantastic, and I can't wait to get into the field to use it." The problem is that various registered training organizations do not stick with a proven sales process; they all pitch a different system of selling and offer too many variations on the theme. Often, after spending a day in a sales course run by a registered training organization, salespeople slip back into old habits because very few sales managers assist with follow-up field coaching.

There are two flaws in the sales training system today. The first is the lack of field sales coaching follow-up on a regular basis. The second is that sales managers seem too busy to follow through with post course field coaching. Some salespeople hate the notion of their manager coming to spend the day with them. Some delight in the assistance, but this should be conducted following product or sales training.

Why pay high costs for in-hours training and then fail to carry out field training follow-up? Companies continue to do this seems to defy common sense.

The selling section in the later part of this book includes several self-critique systems you can include yourself in your normal sales day to double-check on the effectiveness of your last sales call. If we did this well in coaching, sales would increase significantly. Statistics in the United States and locally show that post-selling training and field coaching increase sales by 19 to 21 percent on average.

What Is in It for You as a Salesperson?

Embrace the good sales manager if he or she wishes to introduce a field sales coaching program. Ask yourself, "Is your coach trained to be a coach?" and are they willing to lead the way in selling techniques to show you how it is done—"see one, show one, do one." Many sales managers travel with you but do nothing, offer nothing, and contribute to nothing, partly because they are not formally trained themselves. The good coach will watch your performance and techniques in the field, suggest small constructive improvements to practice, and take it easy with the criticisms. The coach should also teach how you should measure your own sales call performance and critique systems for each sales call. Why? Because they are not with you all the time, and you operate about 95 percent of the time on your own.

Don't be afraid to give feedback to the coach on how the process is working for you. Fully engage yourself in this process for maximum results. If it works, keep it up and enjoy the fruits of your coaching experience. A good coach is great to work with as long as he or she gives you the encouragement and support you really need.

For sales coaches, be prepared to show or demonstrate best practice in the field. Many coaches sit back and judge performance. However, young sales staff want a leader to show them the way.

CHAPTER 2

What the Qualitive Research Confirms

Looking at the Research from an International Perspective

Are we giving all to the job but getting little in return? Chapter 2 deals with the local research compared with research from overseas and the importance of research findings. You will learn to view your role and your corporate workplace from a different corporate perspective.

A recent study published in *New Scientist* 2018, studying workplace stress in Denmark, suggests that throwing yourself into your work you love but not receiving appropriate rewards is a toxic cocktail for biological stress.

What do they mean by the term "biological stress"? The study had two control groups; in one, half the workers did nine to five jobs, and in the other, participants worked longer hours as well as studied a course such as Master of Business Administration (MBA).

The team analyzed cortisol levels in the hair of 100 and 72 salesperson volunteers. Study of the sample cortisol levels shows that this hormone is released in times of stress, helping the body prepare for "fight or flight" by increasing blood sugar levels and slowing down digestion. The study reports chronic stress was found to lead to major health problems. This also leads to other medical problems such as infections and diabetes.

Of all the research that has been done on this very important subject, this particular study serves as the cornerstone of future sales employment staff health and well-being policy.

The research results showed that effort versus reward is a determinant of workplace stress levels. It also showed that levels of cortisol increase if any reward is not forthcoming. Shorter working hours in sales around Scandinavia, such as Sweden, are addressing this very problem.

Research from the Australian Perspective—Is Working in Australia Any Different Than in the United States or Europe?

Getting back to where we started, presenting all this information without supporting my thoughts would be seen as self-indulgent and unrealistic, leaving me open to criticism; besides I would have to defend myself for my Australian research. I set about interviewing people from 40 medical, pharmaceutical, device and critical care companies based in Australia.

Research Method

The interview and data entry process took approximately 18 months. The questionnaire had about 87 questions, encompassing 10 key elements and a 10-point rating scale. Bias was my concern, but I do believe it was only 2 percent.

Results of Australian Research

Research Category

The following 10 categories were used for each research interview.

> Element 1—Personal: *do you believe your company provides care and a safe working place?*
>
> Element 2—Relationships: *how valued and respected are salespeople in our company?*
>
> Element 3—Sales Force: *describe your overall work happiness score for your current sales position?*
>
> Element 4—Management: *do you think your company could do more to keep good sales staff?*
>
> Element 5—Recruiting: *do you think your company has been fully honest when recruiting you?*
>
> Element 6—Training: *could your company do better in product, customer, and sales training?*
>
> Element 7—Incentives and salary: *has your company been honest when paying commission payments?*

Element 8—Performance: *does your company make reasonable efforts to keep high performers?*

Element 9—OHS: *does your company take every opportunity to secure your health and safety?*

Element 10—General: *does your company provide all the tools you need for effective selling?*

I am not sure why, but every time I approached each global pharmaceutical company, I was hurriedly referred to the Legal Department. Yes, they did send me, within a few days, a "no thank you" and "have a great day" response.

For obvious reasons, I have omitted company and individual names; however, being with only a small number of global companies in this industry, an astute individual could short-list and figure out which company I am referring to.

Out of the 10 Category Elements Set Up, No Company Met All the Minimum Criteria That Were Defined

Perhaps only one company in the research field was close, but I was restricted to the national marketing manager for the response. I did back up their responses with relationships within this organization, and, to all intents and purposes, I believe they were close to accurate.

Overall Research Results

Areas of concern found in the research:

- Lying and deception regarding commissions/bonus payments
- Lack of clear understanding and transparency for commission payments
- Lack of personal safety for working after 5 pm and after hours work safety
- Lack of concern for driving long distances and late into the night
- Disconnect between salesperson and management on many levels
- Lack of care and concern for health and welfare

- Distinct lack of strategic sales training and field coaching
- Lack of appropriate product training backed up with product sales training
- Being pulled off own territory to service another territory without recognition
- Management's lack of understanding that sales and field training is paramount
- Recruiters show disregard for openness and transparency of the full job description
- Poor crisis management
- Poor conflict management through human resources
- Working from home and the out of pocket costs
- Salespeople being late for appointments
- Being able to fully trust your representative
- High turnover of representatives
- Lack of respect
- Lack of product knowledge and being too pushy

Research from the Recruitment Point of View

Many companies utilize their own methods of recruitment in-house now. Warranty return of payment for recruiter's services at 3 months is considered too short. Feedback that recruiters do not know enough about the area of expertise is a regular criticism, and the need to place a head as soon as possible is primarily driven by economic reasons.

Pulling Apart the More Concerning Areas of Research, the Following Topics Seem to Show Up More Frequently

Lying and deception from sales managers, lack of care for general safety, significant pressure to meet targets, and the psychological stress ramifications cause salesperson burnout, trust issues, and a high turnover of sales jobs. Other concerning issues that perpetuate continual problems are long working hours, lack of appropriate product and sales training, limited opportunity for advancement above sales level, and conflict resolution within the sales team.

A close review of the short list of job issues shows a more personal undercurrent of trust and how the salesperson is treated. Some companies appear to disconnect at this point, assuming that the salesperson is expendable and can be easily replaced—the "nice knowing you attitude" is what I call it. If you rock the boat, you are tagged and carefully watched, including your communication with other sales colleagues. Please note: your phone call records are scrutinized on a regular basis.

Dismissal Process

Let me escort you out of the building.

One of the most upsetting events that came up in the study is this: You are dismissed, "sacked" from your sales position, and marched out of the premises immediately without being given the opportunity to say goodbye to your colleagues. This behavior has permeated corporate life primarily for "paranoid security" reasons.

Are we becoming insensitive and crass in the way we deal with people? Have we crossed the line of being reasonable to each other? The question should be asked: Have global corporations lost the art of being human?

Global companies have a dismissal policy to follow. The protocol follows the proviso of getting rid of the offending person as quickly and as quietly as possible. I find this policy insensitive and abhorrent. As other employees watch this sacking scenario, trust issues are created and uneasy feelings generated among the remaining staff.

There is a definite need to address this behavior and come up with a more dignified and respectful way of dismissing a sales-person.

Unfair Dismissal

Unfair dismissal has been a bone of contention in every workplace. We are not talking about why, but about how it is carried out. Sheer embarrassment, demoralization, and many other psychological fears arise from this practice. I myself have endured this twice and found this method abhorrent.

I take issue with this process and suggest companies practice a far more respectful method of dismissal. Perhaps allow the person to say goodbye or find some mindful way of saying "thank you for your efforts." It is time to clean up this disgraceful form of behavior.

Use this as a learning exercise and move on. Companies that practice this removal process are afraid of damage to software processes and loss of intellectual property and security, but very few dismissed employees will go to this length to exact revenge.

What of the Future

At the completion of each individual survey, the respondents were asked one final question:

What threats does the sales industry face, and what improvements does the sales industry need for the future?

Threats

Training

Ninety-five percent of the respondents said sales and product training needs greater attention and greater access to personal development and promotional opportunities while going up the corporate ladder for both male and female sales professionals. Concern was expressed over the lack of state and federal health funding along with the currently shrinking industry and the rapid exit of smaller players. Disappearance of the rapport between company management and sales staff and a lack of sales management leadership were also seen as key threats.

Future Individual Needs Uncovered by the Research

- Greater attention to sales and product training
- Improved esteem of the salesperson in the eyes of the customer
- Improved long-term job security
- Applying less stress on sales staff
- Greater appreciation/respect for their sales staff
- Industry to allow companies to compete on a level playing field
- Greater control over unethical behavior and appropriate application of penalties

- Greater honesty and support from the sales manager and the coach
- Sales managers who coach should do a basic training course first (Cert 4 in training and assessment) so they are better trained to teach
- Salespeople should have a business degree or related basic qualification

Positives from the Research

Despite the disappointing results of the study, some positive results did come out of it. Many reported a reasonable satisfaction score with their employer, citing good working conditions, sales managers that did show care and a greater degree of honesty, and a feeling that they belonged to the company.

Please note that saying you're happy in a sales position could be perceived as correct; however, if you know nothing other than this position, your perception could be clouded.

Conclusion from the Research

The list gets very interesting as you drill down. The future is more about personal support for the employees and respect and appreciation than the more business-related needs. Stress played an important part in the future, and lifestyle quality was a very close second.

My question is this: Are we equipped to provide what are seen as very basic needs for salespeople?

Are We a Commodity in Sales Now, and Are We Expendable Too?

My immediate reaction is to say "absolutely," but on second thoughts, many responses are ambiguous. I say yes to the commodity element. Having closely observed management function in global companies, I have noted a syndrome that I describe as "cut the infected section off and grow it again." This is why recruitment companies are always waiting in the wings to fill another sales position. They too well understand that the turnaround in professional sales is about one and a half years, which is great business for them.

The time required to replace the "infected section" is at least around 6 to 12 months, during which the new recruit enters induction and at a significant cost, with only 3-6 months' guarantee back-up support from the recruiting company. Many studies have been published on this recurring problem, but it seems we have fallen into this syndrome of management since the 1970s. I experienced this problem just as it was developing and have noted its progression over the decades. We now see the average retention of salespeople in high-end selling shrinking to 1.8 years or less, with the long-term stints of 10 years or more no longer being the norm.

Professionals working in sales can earn incomes that are well into six figures and are one of the most popular positions companies seek to fill. But retention tends to be low, in view of the pressure to meet sales targets and KPIs, lack of adequate training, and inevitable rejection. Seventy-one percent of companies take 6 months or longer to bring new sales reps on board, and a third of all companies take 9-12 months or more to rescue the position.

Companies have accepted this shorter year turnover as the standard to measure by. This benchmark is built into cost of sales and the price of doing business. Very few global companies look toward a longer retention rate of, for example, 4 years. It is nice to see 5-year service awards being handed out. These longer stints seem to fall into a specialized and rare group, such as:

Survivors in Professional Selling
- Family men needing a regular job and income
- Single women needing security with children
- Older single salespersons wanting regular job security with a home loan
- Salespersons hanging on for promotion
- Salespersons liking their customer base and putting up with internal company politics
- Salespersons who have decided "not" to get involved with internal politics

New salespeople, especially in a technical industry, need strong coaches and mentors to find long-term success.

The Salesperson Constantly on the Look-Out

Known but not talked about much is the salesperson that deliberately seeks another position on a regular basis. There is a specific group that thinks that the more positions they have, the better the curriculum vitae looks. They have recruiters on tap, are continually looking at LinkedIn, and constantly talking to their colleagues about what's going on out there. Is this the "grass is greener over the hill" syndrome, or are they never satisfied with what they have. Salespeople who follow this path will never concentrate fully on their sales job.

I believe this person is primarily seeking attention, feeling they are a precious commodity, and maneuvering themselves into a better paid job position. Perhaps it is ego that drives this personality.

Is it good to do this? No. You get named the "Rep that moves on too soon"; companies steer clear of you when your name continually comes up.

Additional research findings suggest that dissatisfaction with work and promotion aspects of the job as well as thinking of quitting and intending to quit are stages in the turnover process of the salespeople studied. Conversely, variables representing attitude toward searching for another job, attitude toward quitting, and comparison of a perceived alternative job with the present job did not contribute significantly to explaining turnover for the salespeople studied.

Unfortunately, sales managers and leaders also come under criticism for failing to address clear lines of support for their sales team and not being qualified to train their team members. They need to know when and where to apply pressure on the team, including shielding the top-down problem from higher management. The overall outcome of all of these employment issues is that sales management should bear the responsibility of short staff turnover. If sales managers were under less pressure, had the budget for appropriate training and coaching, and spent 2 days inside and 3 days in the field, the figures would change dramatically.[1]

---

[1]Psychosocial work environment and mental health among traveling salespeople Article: 26 Oct 2010—The study followed 1306 salespeople and their health-related issues caused by stress, long hours, short times with companies, and lack of security. The study does reflect the notes discussed in this text. It concludes that if sales managers were less stressed and gave more time to their sales staff, the outcome would be very different, and the problem of shorter turnover would ultimately improve.

CHAPTER 3

Yesterday's versus Today's Sales Environment

Selling back in the seventies to the nineties was simple. You were taught the basics of the product and took it out to customers you thought would buy. The method was uncontrolled and amateurish. Today's selling model requires a great deal of comprehensive application along with sound product training to meet even the basic needs of today's discerning consumer.

Generally, when a company replaces a sales employee during the recruitment process, so much time has elapsed that relevant data, sales, customer notes, and any version of what had transpired between the organization and the customer have long been lost.

During my first training stint, I filled a national sales manager position for a dental company, and part of my role was product training. My skills in training were practically nonexistent, and I was embarrassed to ask for help and so had to use my wits and get on with the job. Fortunately, it worked for me, but I was frustrated that there was no effort to train the trainer.

Record keeping was another clumsy process, and although it did improve with a better card system, it had only one set of records and no backup information for the company, leaving the organization vulnerable when a disgruntled employee decided to leave.

Today's Sales Template

We have at our fingertips an incredible plethora of CRM—Customer Relationship Management—tools, such as digital data recording, customer profile data, a list of where our customers are, how they buy, and their buying patterns. The modern sales professional is given this and more for each sales position, and CRM provides us with a customer listing, full interaction activity, sales records, opportunities, funnel forecasts, and so forth.

So Why Is It Still Difficult to Sell in the Modern Age?

The immediate response to this question is that the competition is so intense, the competitors so cheap, that I'm at a loss to compete.

Company selling support to the global organization is based on forward sales predictions and new product releases. By providing the selling tools just noted, they ask, what else you need to be successful.

The majority of global organizations provide, as you may well know, some pre-appointment job description, selling tools such as a laptop, a phone, a tablet, a car, induction, and basic product familiarization. The practice of throwing him or her the product and seeing what they can do with it is obsolete. Today's global organizations do have a new training process in place, some of which is good, while the rest is not so good.

When we compare our industry with selling new cars, I am told there are only a few car manufacturers who allow their salespeople to begin selling without passing a product sales course first.[1]

In addition, occupation health and safety of sales staff are regarded as a nonexistent subject. Human resources divisions either have nothing to point to in terms of a policy governing the safety of sales staff, selling in the marketplace or show a lack of genuine interest. The case with internal staff, however, presents a completely different scenario. Companies consider the safety of salespeople working at night very low in priority. In the

---

[1]Australian research demonstrates that today's selling environment shows good support for the electronic customer support but lacks company awareness of technical data stress. Recruiters are told that no matter whom they place, the company will provide all necessary digital/communication needs and comprehensive product and sales training. From current research, this is, unfortunately, untrue. Lying and deception are practiced by fabricating the description of a job. In addition, commissions or bonus details are generally not discussed or misrepresented so the compensation schemes can be changed at a moment's notice. Some commission schemes are so complicated that the salesperson is unable to decipher how to calculate what they may earn above base salary.

event of an unfortunate incident resulting in an injury or sexual assault, there would be no "company safety policy" to fall back on; the company would be an easy target for legal or Police action.

Information Overload and How to Avoid the Problem

Do We Manage These Distractions or Not?

When we embark on a new job, we are overloaded with this dilemma, but, eventually, however, we become accustomed to it. Many new salespeople who have been only a week into the job suffer the onset of physical symptoms such as headaches, anxiety, and many more psychological issues. This settles down in time, however, and any festering issues tend to be pushed back into the corners, awaiting an answer in time.

Current research has found that if a salesperson tries to process too much information within a limited time frame, he or she is likely to experience a phenomenon that is termed as salesperson's information overload (SIO), which is detrimental to sales performance. The overload is far greater than what I term "distraction"; it tends to crowd the mind, hampering the performance of the more important functions. Perhaps in a similar way, salesperson burnout could be partly linked. A very good example is the company that has induction stretching over an entire week. After spending the first 2 to 3 days listening to repeated presentations, by Friday your eyes are glazed over, and you're too tired to listen to anything.

I call this temporary information overload, which is generally fixed by a good "stiff drink" and a weekend off. This overload and tiredness are just the forerunner of complete information overload. It is important to recognize these initial symptoms and prepare or avoid the cause. One good practice is not to look at your personal Facebook messages and so on during the day, as this only adds to the technical overload you don't need. You can carry a second phone to avoid this incessant problem.[2]

---

[2]Why some people seem to suffer more than others—Ruud Janssen, Henk de Poot Telematica Institute. Jensen confirms information overload is a widely recognized problem worldwide, caused by too much work, work frequency, constant interruptions, and too many devices to use at once.

Information Overload—Here Are Some Symptoms to Look Out for

- **The salesperson is often confused** because he or she has access to too much information.
- **The prospect is confused** because scientific research proves that humans simply cannot process excess information, especially if it is not logically structured, takes too long, or is unclear.
- **The worst situation** is that the overloaded sales person is unable to tell important and necessary information from excessive fluff. As a result, the salesperson struggles with the task of bringing important information to the table during a sales discussion and alienates the customer very quickly.
- The overloaded salesperson may suffer a breakdown in their professional or personal lives.
- Too much work is expected of you.
- Are they able to identify what is most important to the prospect and present a strong, unique solution that will meet their greatest need?

I would go so far as to say that all of us in professional sales today are suffering sales information overload. How we categorize items of information according to their relative importance is up to us. If you can't do this, seek help from your sales leader to distinguish what is important and what is not.

To provide a rosy picture of today's sales environment, especially around global selling companies, is just short of disgraceful. Admittedly, there are many companies that try harder than others, but when speaking to research interviewees, one finds that the story is astonishingly different than one imagines.

Some companies do get it right. Research demonstrates that their employees show a higher than normal degree of satisfaction than their competitive players.

Salesperson Respect in Today's Industry

Have we improved the image of the modern professional corporate seller?

Having dealt with various doctors over the last 49 years, I would describe the early experience as a "tenuous relationship." During the

1980s and 1990s, respect for salespeople did improve as the industry was advancing rapidly in technology. This did undergo a setback during the pharmaceutical time of Doctors complaining about poor conduct and, unfortunately, the poor respect issue rubbed off on the surgical device sector too.

For example, the introduction of CT/MRI scanning, anesthesia, implantable devices, stapling, vascular stents, improved catheter design for neuro, and new drug therapies has generated widespread interest. The explosion of such technology created a need for the physician and surgeon to rely more on product application advice, and the entry of clinical nurses into the profession demonstrated a higher need for qualified salespeople.

Many sales teams currently have a mix of account managers, who are responsible for the business end, and a team of technical skilled experts ready and waiting to cooperate with trials, installations, and technical advice. This symbiosis of various skills works well if the lines of responsibility are clear and adhered to.

So with All This History Have We Improved Our Image?

Absolutely "yes." Technology is changing so fast that the time available for operators to keep up with product advancement **is limited**. Having an experienced sales person keeping the operator up to date with current advancements is still appreciated, but users want clear and open answers to their questions. This builds respect for us in that we are seen as knowledgeable advisors and as a valuable resource in their vital work.

Respect in the Hospital Environment Now—As an Example

This relationship has changed significantly in the medical industry. If you are not dealing with doctors, you will be dealing with nursing staff, generally senior-level, technical staff such as biomedical engineers, radiology staff, and chemotherapy staff, project managers, supply chain, DON, (Director of Nursing), CFO, CEO levels, and so on. Operating theaters are a very different area to work in and require a holistic approach. In general, the decision makers are well coached to deal with "reps" and have specific controls on what to say and how much time they can spend with you. In some cases, there are specific restrictions on visiting these customers and how to access them. The respect for our profession is good, but the intense number of sales calls on all customers is said to be too much, so you can understand the cutback on the time they have for consultation.

In other aspects of sales, respect is earned individually depending on salesperson behavior and professionalism along with company policy.

Trait Test: Take This Test to See How You Stack Up

The purpose of this test is to bring forward your traits needed to function as a productive salesperson. It is important to answer the questions honestly. There is the obvious answer for every question, but read them carefully before you answer.

Trait 1: Understands the product

1. Takes the time to understand the product so he or she can see whether it solves a prospect's problem.
2. Talks about how wonderful the product is without knowing whether it's even relevant to a prospect.

Answer: 1. or 2.

Trait 2: Always learning

1. Seeks ways to fine-tune and advance their skills.
2. Thinks he doesn't need more help after learning the basics.

Answer: 1. or 2.

Trait 3: Are you open to feedback?

1. Seeks feedback from their peers and managers.
2. Thinks everyone is out to get him.

Answer: 1. or 2.

Trait 4: Understands business goals and the company's larger picture

1. Understands the goals of the company and how he fits into the bigger picture.
2. Could not care less about the company and only wants to collect a paycheck.

Answer: 1. or 2.

Trait 5: High ethical standards

1. Wants to work with people who have high ethical standards and take their work seriously.
2. Justifies any action with an "I'll do anything to get the deal" attitude.

Answer: 1. or 2.

Trait 6: Persistence

1. Is persistent, but not annoying.
2. Thinks persistence means calling a prospect several times a day.

Answer: 1. or 2.

Trait 7: Knows when it's a no

1. Understands that hearing "no" will let him move on.
2. Wants to continue to chase deals that don't have a chance of being sealed.

Answer: 1. or 2.

Trait 8: Always exceeding

1. Sets goals for himself that exceed the expectations of the company or his manager.
2. Is done as soon as he hits his quota.

Answer: 1. or 2.

Trait 9: Listens

1. Listens carefully
2. Talks and avoids seeking customer needs

Answer: 1. or 2.

Trait 10: Builds their reputation

1. Realizes there are ways to game the system, but knows doing so would hurt his or her reputation and the company's.
2. Finds any shortcut available and keeps it to themselves.

Answer: 1. or 2.

Trait 11: Targets the buyer

1. Quickly identifies who can make a buying decision about a product before doing a full pitch.
2. Pitches anyone at a company who will listen.

Answer: 1. or 2.

Trait 12: Knows what's needed

1. Knows when to stop talking.
2. Talks himself out of a deal that was already sealed.

Answer: 1. or 2.

Trait 13: Ongoing dialogue

1. Takes feedback from her manager, but also provides feedback to his manager so that they both can grow.
2. Hates the word "management" and thinks everyone needs to be looking out only for himself.

Answer: 1. or 2.

Trait 14: Calm under pressure

1. Understands rejection is part of the job and remains calm and cool even if the person on the other end of the phone isn't pleasant.
2. Tries to fight fire with fire and gets into a verbal debate that leads nowhere.

Answer: 1. or 2.

Trait 15: Honest

1. Is honest even if it could cost him or her the sale.
2. Leaves out information that he fears the prospect may not want to hear.

Answer: 1. or 2.

Trait 16: Pride in the role

1. Respects himself or herself and takes pride in his profession.
2. Does not really want to do sales.

Answer: 1. or 2.

Do you recognize any of these good or bad sales traits in yourself?

If you are answering these questions honestly, you should be altering your selling behavior or talking to your coach for advice on how to alter bad traits.

CHAPTER 4

Bullying in Sales & What Motivates the Lying Boss

Introduction

In this chapter, we discuss how bullying affects salespeople and how it takes a toll on their personal lives and mental health. While reviewing this, we discuss ways of dealing with the lying boss and what motivates people to enact such behaviors. Pathological lying (also called *pseudologia fantastica* and mythomania) is habitual or compulsive lying and was first described in the medical literature in 1891 by Anton Delbrueck.

Bullying in Sales

Definition

Workplace bullying is ongoing harmful or threatening behavior by a person or group of people in your workplace that creates a risk to your health and safety. It takes the form of repeated harmful remarks and attacks or making fun of your work or of you as a sales person (including your family, sex, sexuality, gender identity, race or culture, education, or economic background).

During my career in sales, I have experienced only one personal bullying episode, which lasted 3 months. It caused great stress to myself and my family until I left the company. Back then the laws were not so strict and possibly unsupportive of the bullied person. I have seen others being bullied several times, and often it was a female sales person at the receiving end.

It has always surprised me whenever a person being bullied in the workplace has been reluctant to take the matter further to human resources or an outside ombudsman.

If you think you are being bullied at work by your sales manager or team sales member, you should be aware of the following indicators:

- being less active or successful in selling, your sales results begin to decline
- being less confident about prospecting sales, less likely to engage new customers
- feeling scared, stressed, anxious, or depressed, ending up with a clinical depression
- often having time off because of stress-related illness, using up all of your sick leave
- your life outside of work affected, for example, study, relationships, staying at home more often
- wanting to stay away from work, using up all personal sick leave
- feeling like you can't trust your employer or the people with whom you work in a team
- lacking confidence and happiness about yourself and your sales job, loss of self-esteem
- physical signs of stress such as headaches, backaches, sleep problems, other illnesses are more critical to deal with
- feeling nobody in the company will listen to you, causing you to withdraw

To make a complaint in your country, enter the word bullying in Google and follow the appropriate links.

How to Resolve Bullying Directly

If you are being bullied, howsoever subtly, by a work colleague in the sales team, or elsewhere, then please follow these suggestions.

I have always believed in going directly to the source of the problem. Confront the offending person, though perhaps not at work. Ask their reasons for such behavior, and wait for a reply; be silent till you hear a response. If the person says nothing, then express your dissatisfaction with their behavior, and explain that they are out of line and must cease their bullying activity. If, however, the response to your question is of an aggressive nature, as, for instance, "you deserve it," then ask why. If you disagree, then say, "If you do not desist from this bullying behavior, I will take this to our sales manager and human resources." Generally, this quells the situation, but there are some people that resist advice and persist with the offending behavior.

If you record the conversation, kindly inform the other party of the recording being taken.

Responsibility of Employers

Your employer has a legal responsibility under the Occupational Health and Safety and Anti-discrimination law to provide a safe workplace. Employers have a duty of care for your health and well-being while at work. This is current in many Western countries, including America, Europe, United Kingdom, Australia, New Zealand, and Canada. An employer who allows bullying to occur in the workplace is probably not adhering to state legislation. Be aware that in many cases the bullying is their word against yours. Going to senior management without evidence is difficult, but you still have the law on your side.

The Workplace Bullying Institute in the USA, stated that 55 percent of the US population have experienced or witnessed bullying (Wales IAWBH Conference 2010). The author, Mr. Glen Worthington, gave a speech in Denmark about the amount of bullying in the workplace. The statistics varied from 15 to over 50 percent according to what study was published. My own estimate, based on personal experience, would be around 20 percent in the sales workplace, citing jealousy, underperformers, personal dislike, and accusations of a salesperson not pulling his or her weight.

With all the current legislation provided to employees now, it is surprising that bullying is still prevalent today. It is a behavior we should all be vigilant of.[1]

Lying and Deception

As stated in my introduction, lying and deception was common (20 to 30 years ago), and is sadly common now. Even dealing with global

---

[1] Are Sales Teams Bullying CPG Senior Management to Reject Change? By Tool Box, Jun 29, 2016.

companies, with all their processes and code of ethics statements, the research cited this answer time and again: "I was told this, but when I got into the job it appeared very different than I understood." Surprisingly, 90 percent of my research respondents agreed the information about the job function, training, remuneration, and commissions were either different, untrue, or deceitful.

This same issue was put to the HR recruiters in the survey, and all said they were unaware of this deception. Are the recruiters also being deceptive to save the embarrassment of being challenged, or are the recruiters deceiving themselves? I think I would consider both. One thing I am sure about is that recruiters go to a specific level of questioning regarding whom they offer and place a head. My research showed this information was lacking in detail; in fact, recruiters provided very vague answers.

The sales organization is doing nothing illegal by lying. In fact, one might conclude that these acts of management deception are no more than **"white lies,"** although there may certainly be benefits for employees lying in the workplace, according to some. For me, having a manager who lied wasn't so much of an issue as figuring out how to make him or her stop the lying behavior.

If you are subjected to a lying boss, then get your facts right before you confront them. Trust your gut feeling to determine initially what was wrong.

Both these references convey a clear message that corporations within or outside will lie to varying degrees. This has been demonstrated with recent fabrications of truth among car manufacturers regarding emissions claims. The concerning fact that management will tell lies to employees if the company needs protection is a concerning part of corporate sales.

Exposing Your Boss as a Liar, and What I Should Do

Better to make an appointment with your boss, not at work but somewhere neutral. Firstly, when you meet up, take time to gauge the bosses' demeanor, and then begin the discussion. If the boss is "evasive," then start with a general conversation around sales and so on.

Bring up your grievance then stop talking to see how he or she responds. When there is a possibility of bringing down a boss for lying, have your evidence ready at hand and in writing such as an e-mail or diary note.

If he or she argues, saying, "I forgot this" or "Did we talk about this?" or "I have overlooked this, sorry," and if there is contrition, then give them the benefit of the doubt and request a rectification of the misunderstanding and setting this in writing. However, if the response is negative and resistant and they argue that you are wrong, then bring out the evidence. Please remember not to bring out the evidence at first but to use it if you need it. If there is still an indignant refusal to acknowledge the lie, then plan B is in order.

You have a choice of several options. Utilize contact with human resources, but again I urge you to be concise and analytical about your grievance. Try to take the emotion out of your discussion with human resources, and stick to the facts. Request a resolution immediately.

Note that human resources will schedule a meeting between you and the lying party to discuss and resolve the deadlock. In general, human resources will be on the side of management, but look for a satisfactory settlement without compromising your integrity.

If your grievance is of the nature of a sexual assault, the police are the only port of call for a report and action. Yes, report the assault, but follow the police with their advice.

Understanding Intentions behind Your Boss's Behavior and Watching Out for These Following Tell-Tale Signs

What are some examples of boss lying?

- Your boss says that if you do well this year in sales, you will be up for a promotion.
- Your boss says your commission rate is 1.5 percent of overall sales, but it is really 1 percent.
- Your boss continually says he or she will come out in the field with you soon.
- Your boss commits to a pay raise above CPI but gives only 1 percent increase.

- Your boss promises you a new car next month, but 5 months go by and nothing materializes.
- Your boss promises you an overseas educational trip but never makes good on the commitment.
- Your boss promises a family trip to Fiji if you are 10 percent over budget but never makes good on the promise.
- Your boss promises a drink at the end of a great sales week but never comes.

These are just a few of the great many lies bosses make every day. Small promises progress to larger fabrications of lying and eventually fall apart.

What is Lying is a form of deceptive planning and alternative strategy or a misrepresentation, distortion, or equivocation. Some call this scamming or being dodgy. The individual that lies consistently is generally deficient in a particular personal or work skill or wants to be seen to be far better than he or she really is. We know that the web of deception eventually catches up with them and they are exposed for their fabrications of the truth. The problem for the salesperson is that you have lost all respect.

Strange Behavior

The moment your boss starts to behave strangely or tries to lie to you, it is necessary to know the actual intentions of the behavioral changes. These strange behavioral patterns could be that he or she may be managing you out of the company or trying to hide something they are doing that is against company policy. It could also be that he or she may be having an affair with a sales colleague and thinks you know too, or performing dodgy deals, or is conscious of overcompensation of promises they can't keep.

Reasons behind the Boss's Lying Behavior

It is impossible to understand the reason behind constant lying patterns, especially of someone in a leadership position. Is it only a case of the manager being under pressure, or is there a personality deficiency at work? The boss could be feeling threatened, for example, if a bright young sales person is stripping up sales better than the boss did. The lying problem starts small, with perhaps one individual receiver, but escalates into a spiral of lying and ends up as a major lie to manage.

Delivering Empty Promises

Sales managers sometimes make promises that they are unable to keep. This could be a reward for high monthly sales over and above commission, for example, a dinner out with your partner, or a trip overseas for outstanding effort but not running this by management approval for such a promise. The reason behind such behavior is that the individual boss is looking for improved or additional sales to finish up for the month or year. Alternatively, they may want to be seen as a great leader.

Management Skills Will Be Poor

A boss who lies constantly can never handle difficult situations in a positive manner but may take advantage of such situations and cash in as part of their personal agenda. This behavior would, for example, favor other salespeople, alienate you in the sales team, hinder your chances of contributing to sales team decisions, and avoid your opinions. Some sales managers lacking certain management skills will cover up their poor skills by putting the responsibility onto the team members but taking the full credit. To me as a sales person, a manager taking credit for a good sale when you did all the work embodies the worst of management behavior. This in itself is the most demoralizing behavior a sales person will ever experience.

Managing You Out

A very common reason for all of this irrational behavior is that the boss, either under instructions or on their own, is purposely managing you out. Let's think of this carefully. If your sales are poor for, say, more than 3 to 4 months and you do not make budget or, say, meet only 50 percent of plan, you should expect a tap on the shoulder: "Why are sales bad?" In my opinion, if you have not received a first or second warning by now, including an offer of retraining or assistance, then the company is in breach of its obligations to assist you.

A Final Word of Advice

During your career, you will undoubtedly encounter a lying sales colleague or boss; this is inevitable. How you go about dealing with this unacceptable behavior is a question of your personal ethics and values. Always be on the alert for this behavior, and when you encounter it make notes in your diary for future reference. Having a record is imperative for future use. If the lying persists, follow my method in regard to how to confront the liar.

Prima Donna Management—What Drives the Prima Donna?

I must say I am guilty of this problem, so I can talk about this with some experience. Being the top salesperson in many global companies can make you egotistical and prone to expect the respect that comes with this title. Most of the time, you just want respect and compliments for the sales you have achieved. In some ways you are referred to from your company as a leader to look up to. Other sales members want to exceed your achievements and try to emulate your style.

When it comes to sales team management, sales managers i know have a love–hate relationship with the prima donnas in their sales teams. They love the star player's passion and hard work, while they loathe the self-centered behaviors that demoralize or discourage the rest of the team.

That leaves sales managers with a dilemma. If they come down hard on a prima donna, that salesperson may just take his her talents elsewhere. But a sales manager can't afford to ignore the situation, either, as prima donnas are often engaged in behaviors that are detrimental to the team and can sometimes take the sales boundaries to the limits.

A simple truth in sales management is that "what you don't confront, you condone." As it turns out, many sales managers admit that they have taken a hands-off approach with their prima donna salespeople, leaving them alone for weeks or months at a time. "Hands off" is a nicer way of saying, "lack of management." These are common management mistakes.

Sales managers will also admit that they often don't communicate expectations or set standards on anything other than production results. And remember, a "standard" becomes a standard only if you coach to it on an ongoing basis. So, naturally, your top producers (and everyone else on the team) will come to think that sales production is the only thing you care about. From the salesperson perspective, I would look toward the prima donna and learn anything worth learning. Look at the prima donna's relationship with their customers; do they have the trust of the customer, and how do they close on the customer? Look at their planning for their territory. Try to weed out the bull, and look for any selling techniques you can adopt, not the bad ones.[2]

Worst Lies That Salespeople Tell Their Bosses

When we are young and less confident in sales, we often take two lines to reply to the boss's questions. Of course, it depends very much on the attitude of the boss too, but we have a choice to make.

- Smoothing things over (white lie response).
- Being up front and honest.

These two actions will form the basis of your learning phase and will build the character of the type of salesperson you will be all your life.

These are some of the typical lies that sales people use.

- The budget is not an issue.
- I have a great memory, so I don't need to use CRM.
- I made 20 cold calls today.
- We lost that deal because marketing was not providing support.
- I will close all my deals by quarter end.
- My phone battery was flat, sorry, so I was unable to return your call.
- These are all qualified opportunities. Truth: Some must be more qualified than others.

---

[2]March 25, 2011—Managing a Prima Donna Salesperson/The paper shows how to work with a sales prima donna and how to manage such a sales person in the team.

- My CRM was down today—sorry.
- My car has broken down, so I will have to work from home.
- It's a qualified lead, but they have no money.
- I am working from home this morning.
- I know the lead buyer personally; he is a good friend.
- These new leads just advanced right before this funnel review meeting, so I don't have all the details. Truth: You're not on top of your accounts.

Remember that when we tell lies, your boss has probably done the same.

OK, why do we bring up these routine fibs all the time? There are things happening in your life apart from work, so sometimes we have to tell a white lie to cover time off without taking leave. I have always formed a very basic view: If you are doing OK with sales and your boss is a good supporter, be honest and say, "I need some personal time off, please." You may be surprised they will be OK with this rather than finding out you were lying. Remember, one lie to your boss puts you in the _watch_ category.

Let's Look at the Various Versions of Lying

White Lies versus Habitual Lying

A white lie is said to be harmless or trivial, especially when it is aimed at avoiding hurting someone's feelings or hiding one's actions. Are the lies we are telling our bosses considered "white lies" or behaviors that are far more serious? From your boss's point of view, they may be conditioned to hearing an occasional white lie or two, but if you are continuously practicing this behavior to avoid being transparent about what you are not doing, then it becomes habitual. The white lie is the most popular recourse at work and has become part of regular and routine communication. I am not saying this is right!

Four Lies We Use in Selling

When you look at the following four types of lies, how far do you go to do your job?

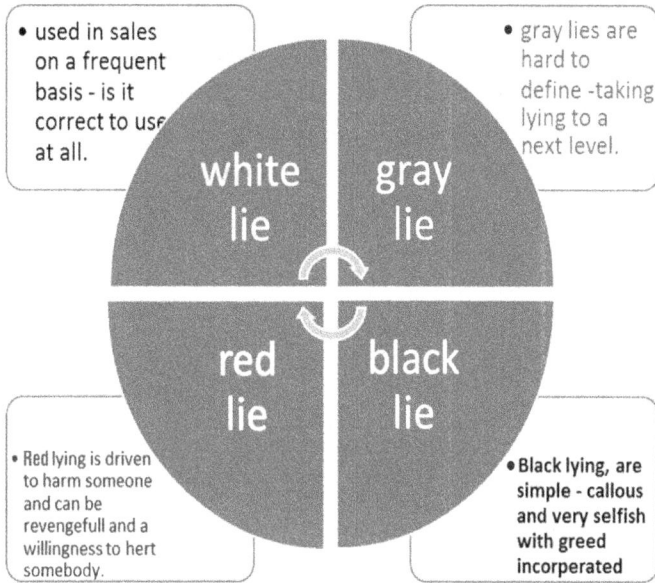

- used in sales on a frequent basis - is it correct to use at all.

- gray lies are hard to define -taking lying to a next level.

white lie

gray lie

red lie

black lie

- Red lying is driven to harm someone and can be revengefull and a willingness to hert somebody.

- Black lying, are simple - callous and very selfish with greed incorperated

Figure 4.1 The 4 lies in sales

The following four types of lies are described here

White lies: In this model, white lies are altruistic as we seek first to help others, even at some cost to ourselves. In practice, there are numerous shades of white, and what we tell ourselves are white lies often tend more toward gray than pure white. It is up to you and your ethics to decide how far you take the white lie. Always remember that continual white lies become habitual. White lies develop from childhood and evolve from there.

Gray lies: Most of the lies we tell are gray lies and are aimed partly at helping others and partly at helping ourselves. They may vary in the shade of gray, depending on the balance of help and harm. Gray lies are, almost by definition, hard to clarify. For example, you can lie to help a sales friend out of trouble but then gain the reciprocal benefit of them lying for you while those they have harmed in some way lose out. Using gray lies further adds to the perpetual circle of lying.

Black lies: Black lies are about simple and callous selfishness. We tell black lies when others gain nothing, and the sole purpose is either to get ourselves out of trouble (reducing harm against ourselves) or to gain something we desire (increasing benefits for ourselves). The worst black lies are very harmful for others.

Red lies: Red lies are about spite and revenge. They are driven by the motive of harming others, even at the expense of harming oneself. They may even be malicious, dangerous, and illegal.

Why Should We Accept Lying in the Corporate World?

There is a degree of acceptability in all situations, so I am told. What is acceptable to one and then another can be very different. Fundamentally, your upbringing will play greatly on this concept. If you are consistently lied to and if you have overlooked the principles of people that lie, then you will be more likely to accept even the black or red lie.

As an ethical and honest salesperson, I would only accept the truth, not even a white lie!

Start your day with a clear head, and fully honest, it makes you feel better.

CHAPTER 5

Personal Problems We Encounter in Sales

The objective of this chapter is to discuss the more difficult personal problems we encounter in sales—belief in yourself, burnout and how to recognize it, tips on how to deal with stress, and other psychological issues. Of all the subjects in this book, I believe these are the most important to address and recognize.

Belief in Yourself—How Important Is This Concept?

In the end, we are all driven to make sales. It is our emotional approach to this very important task that sorts the performers from the nonperformers. The following nine triggers are keys to understanding yourself better as a seller.

<u>Please identify whether you have any of the following feelings about your current job?</u>

- **Belief in Yourself:** The most important fundamental selling need over all other skills you have
- **Belonging:** A strong desire to belong to something such as a sales team, this can be traced back to infancy
- **Fear:** Used as a marketing tactic for loyalty but holds a powerful trigger for job security
- **Guilt:** The most puritanical of all emotions, related to deep psychological issues; are you being honest at work and to yourself?
- **Trust:** Trust is what you should be aiming for, but can you be trusted too?

- **Leadership:** The driver behind long-term sales; is your leader inspiring enough for you to want to work hard for them?
- **Values:** Do you operate in sales with your values or principles foremost in mind before your company?
- **Gratification**—when we don't get what we want, the psychological response is anxiety or tension. Are you getting gratification from your work?
- **Belief in Your Product**—if you don't have belief in your product, do not attempt to sell it at all.

If you say I have all of the feelings listed, I would suggest that you seek help from a professional immediately. It is good to look at this list and say, "I relate to some of these feelings about my job." You should, in general, align closely with trust, values, and belief in yourself, and product knowledge as a starting point.

Belief in Yourself...

Undoubtedly, this is the most important trait we need for professional sales. Say it to yourself every morning and night. At the worst of times, such as low sales periods, keep saying it. As a leader, belief in yourself is paramount. Your staff are constantly observing you and your leadership skills, looking for the ultimate confidence. Your self-belief is essential for motivation and leadership.

"I Believe in Myself"

Look at others in your sales team and ask yourself who are those members that have a high belief and those that have a low belief in themselves? The belief in yourself is a continual practice and needs ongoing reinforcement each day. It is an inner feeling that only you can feel and gives you a reason to push on regardless. A word of warning, if I may: If you need to say continually, "I believe in myself," you should question yourself. Salespeople with low self-esteem will not be successful, and may need to find a job elsewhere.

Of all the personal traits I have (good and bad), i have always believed in myself. This trait or quality is to be the most important life skill to inherit from your parents. Parents hand down this quality to you to practice and play out during your life. If you did not have this quality handed down, try the following exercise.

- Practice your product knowledge and start to like learning.
- Practice your selling skills, and be prepared to alter behavior.
- Practice your delivery presentation skills.
- Take a good look at your appearance so as to fit into your sales environment.
- Take on a mentor for ongoing improvement, and set out a program to follow.
- Finally, practice ethical sales so you do not have to defend untruths.

Interestingly, I have never been asked during an interview, "Do you believe in yourself?"

Additional Behavioral Learning to Try

Practice the following behavioral suggestions. On realizing certain traits, you need to work on the following suggestions that you may want to continue to practice:

- Push past your discomfort barrier, overcome it, and believe in yourself.
- Put yourself out there, and be "OK" with not knowing whether people will accept you.
- Stick to a habit, not listening to the negative self-talk that normally holds you back.
- Learn to trust yourself and your personal judgment, knowing you will make mistakes.
- Never give in and never give up; the sales will happen.
- Learn through repeated attempts that it's OK to fail, that you can be OK in failure.

- Learn through repeated experiments that you are stronger than you think and that you are more capable and more tolerant of discomfort than you think.
- If the sale falls through, get up the next day fresh and ready to go again.
- Remember your customers will see this belief in you.

Failure as a Behavioral Issue

Failure is not a personal fault. It is a very normal human behavior we learn from childhood. You can fail several times doing a task, but, in the end, you must master it. This is called behavioral learning. Surprisingly, this learning phase continues through our normal life.

Example of Failing to Learn

You have made an appointment with a customer to sell a new product. You take a cursory look at the new product the night before. Your sales manager is also attending the sales call with you. Over a cup of coffee prior to the sales call, you both discuss the forthcoming meeting strategy and come up with a close option for the customer, whom you know very well.

The sales call proceeds reasonably, but the customer is not convinced and fails to give you an order. What has gone wrong? Obviously, lack of preparation.[1]

Pushing on No Matter What

The best advice I can give you is to focus on the end game outcome: What do I need to do to achieve this goal, and what assistance do I need for its execution?

---

[1]The concept of pushing on regardless comes from digging deep and convincing yourself, "tomorrow is a new day and new opportunity," and if you try hard enough sales will happen.

To Improve Your Overall Performance, Review the Following Basic Sales Suggestions

- Know your sales budget for each month in dollars and units.
- Plan the opportunities that will achieve the monthly sales you need.
- Appoint or see the customers as "low-hanging fruit" to achieve the immediate sales.
- Take time out to review medium to long sales funnel opportunities.
- Critically look at the timelines for order entry.
- Think about whom you need to pull into the sales project to help you.
- Plan the project phase and timeline of customer engagement.
- Accept sales deadlines as a pivotal end to the objective.
- Obsess less about this, and believe in your planning and sales abilities.
- Be prepared to work hard, and put in the hours needed for success.
- Believe in yourself to achieve good sales.
- Always be on guard for new business opportunities.

In the end, I can't tell you how to believe in yourself, as it comes from doing the job well; follow the preceding list, and self-belief will come automatically. Practicing selling, reviewing the sales, and accepting coaching are key to the evolution of this belief.

Personal quote _____

Many people have asked me over the years, "How come you are so confident and get the sale so easy?" Little do they know that I am generally a shy person and can suffer a high degree of anxiety at times. It has taken me many years to develop a positive self-belief, and it has come not from attending personality development training courses but from sheer determination to be successful. The confidence tends to just follow on behind and develop along the way. There is a reason for promoting and selling these programs, and that is money and profit.

Burnout and the Medical Implications for You and the Company

The sales profession has its own unique kind of stress, and it should be easy to spot when you're on **anxiety overload**. These signs are not always clear from the start but can creep up on you over months or years. Everyone experiences some of these signs in their work from time to time, but if you're feeling several of them on a regular day-to-day basis, you're heading for burnout, and you need to seek professional help.

Look at the following list and pick out what symptom is close to what you may be experiencing now.

- **Indifference**—lost a sale, and you're not even that bothered by it, feeling no loss
- **Malaise**—having a hard time getting motivated to do anything
- **Dog-sees-squirrel syndrome**—you're easily distracted, missing key selling
- **Regular illness** and at the doctor's regularly
- **Spinning your wheels**—you feel like you're working harder and not getting anywhere.
- **Losing a big sale** and not recovering back to work as you should the next day
- **Snapping at your team members/boss** and losing your temper for no reason
- **Starting to look at other jobs** to solve the immediate problem
- **Not recognizing** your personal and private home issues
- **Having serious health problems** associated with stress.

If the preceding list bothers you, then take stock and ask yourself, "How close am I to burnout?"

I have been in the same situation of spinning my wheels; did I have burnout or not? I think I did, and I consulted my mentor to help me with the situation. Breaking this mindset is difficult. Recognizing the symptoms and identifying the particular reason is even harder; this is where having a mentor comes in handy.[2]

---

[2]Please note, some better companies offer anonymous psychological counseling, whereby your name or details are withheld from the employer. This should be included in your employment agreement and contact numbers attached. I have availed myself of this service and found it helpful.

10 Suggestions to Overcome Sales Burnout and Stress for Sales Professionals

Exercise: pick out any of the examples and notate for future review.

- Pace yourself. Stop getting pulled in twenty different directions. Prioritize your time and efforts. Get rid of "excess baggage" projects.
- Call it a night a little earlier than usual. Getting more sleep is a surefire way to help the mind and give up alcohol for 3 months.
- Exercise and eat healthier, limit the caffeine to two cups per day, drink more water.
- See your doctor for medical advice; you may have depression also and be in need of treatment.
- Surround yourself with positive people and activities. Helping, serving others is also a great way to "lose yourself" and keep the burnout under control.
- Buy some new business clothes… shoes, shirt/blouse, anything. Feeling good about your appearance really does help get yourself out of the fog. Also, getting a haircut, style, or color change can help. Get a new look!
- Spend time with your family and friends—get back to your "roots," so to speak.
- Get some sunshine in your life. Get outside, where there's sun and fresh air, even a holiday.
- Work on a short-term list of personal and work objectives you want to achieve, and post a reminder in your Outlook for review.

Taking steps to reduce burnout is simple, but when the individual wants to address it, the problem can be overwhelming. Going to the right doctor for the medical issues, having a good mentor to consult, and making an objective short-term list are a great beginning.

Please note that the quick fix for burnout doesn't come quickly; it takes months to recover, so plan a simple list of recovery activities, and work your way through it slowly.

What If None of This Is Working?

Assuming there's nothing clinically wrong … If you're still having issues, then perhaps it's time for a new position, possibly a new company. However, if you are going to travel down this path, look at the reasons why a company move is in order, and list them.

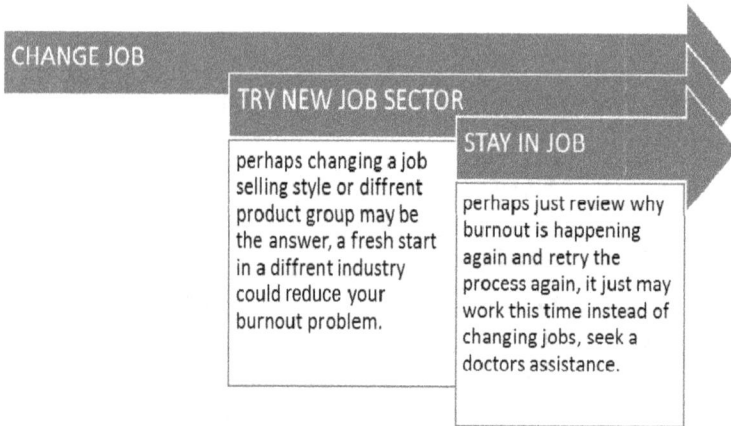

CHANGE JOB

TRY NEW JOB SECTOR

perhaps changing a job selling style or diffrent product group may be the answer, a fresh start in a diffrent industry could reduce your burnout problem.

STAY IN JOB

perhaps just review why burnout is happening again and retry the process again, it just may work this time instead of changing jobs, seek a doctors assistance.

Figure 5.1 Steps to check off when leaving your position

Distinguishing Salesperson Burnout versus Stress

Commissions, quotas, competition—Many factors trigger stress in the daily life of a salesperson. By nature, salespeople find themselves in situations that create a high-stress environment. While some of that stress is good, it's also likely to have a negative impact on the productivity of each individual sales team member and his or her daily activities.

We all deal with stress differently, but there are a few techniques that every salesperson can apply to cope with stressful situations, while keeping their composure and continuing to close deals. Most people experience stress, but there is a difference between regular stress and burnout, which is mental, physical, and emotional exhaustion.

Burnout Starts as a Normal Stress Response

The limbic system prepares us for fight or flight when we meet with a difficult emergency. Often, we don't need this primitive response as we're not actually in flight or fleeing from a physical threat. But the limbic system doesn't discriminates. So it creates physiological arousal such as heart racing, shorter breath, muscle tension, and periods of severe anxiety. This can lead to burnout, a constant state of stress for a prolonged time, and placing unnecessary pressure on the limbic and adrenal system. You may not be aware that it is happening, but your body and mind do, so listen to them more often.

Burnout can lead to severe depression and anxiety. Periods of excessive and prolonged stress can also manifest physically and cause health to deteriorate. Along with headaches, memory impairment, and respiratory and gastrointestinal infections, burnout can cause sleep disturbance and suppress immunity. A simple cold or flu can end up in far more serious medical conditions. The end result is that working in sales while suffering burnout results in sales decline.

Tips to Pick Stressors

The biggest stressor most salespeople face is the constant pressure to meet overly optimistic activity and funnel sales goals. Can you really make 10 sales appointments in a day? When the expectations are too high, sometimes sales calls can feel like high-stakes, make-or-break moments. Additional stressors develop from low sales results vis-à-vis those of other team members. Pressure from upper management to meet sales targets and not really knowing your sales funnel properly adds to the overall stressors.

Is there a Solution?

Take an honest look at your data before setting hard sales targets. To gain an even deeper understanding of the marketplace, business owners should get firsthand experience generating sales themselves so they know what to expect from their sales team. You and the sales manager should be out in the marketplace, coaching and being closely involved in the day-to-day business. This process in itself shares the market load and creates an engagement between your boss and you.[3]

---

[3]How to deal With Stress in Sales/Pub November 23, 2016 by Nick Hedges. Nick Hedges discusses the same issues we have dealt with, stress being the precursor to burnout.

Care for General Safety in Sales

Many global companies demonstrate an overall disappointing attitude and lack of care for professional salespeople, primarily in regard to health and safety and training.

Every research respondent highlighted this overall lack of care from his or her management team. The word "safety" was in some cases interpreted differently, but, generally, respondents aligned it with their own care and safety at work.

Taking time off for illness, in general, presented no problem, with the obligatory 10 sick leave days allowed in most countries. Additional sick leave, if needed, was negotiated between the sales manager and the individual. However, working late at night, driving home late at night after visiting customers, attending conferences, and getting home late were the most common concerns raised.

Let me share some of my own experiences:
On two occasions working late at night in an operating theater for one of the major Melbourne hospitals, I made my way to the adjacent car park and found people shooting up drugs near my car. On other occasions, a female work colleague worked in an intensive care unit late at night, and requested assistance to the car park at 2 a.m. to go home. This is a common situation for medical trials as patients come through at any time and require company technical advice and guidance for "go live procedures". Many times, my colleague tried to request hospital security to accompany her to the adjacent car park, but they were often too busy in the emergency department.

This issue of safety was raised not only with sales management but also with human resources by many employees of the company. Unfortunately, there were frustrating replies: "Finish up earlier" or "wait for security to help you." This is not feasible and showed a clear lack of understanding of how business requires us to do what we need to do and a lack of care from higher management. In my opinion it is a disgrace.

In my case, on two occasions I wrote to human resources requesting a written policy on this very issue, and the reply was "we do not have a written policy to give you." No further discussion was offered, and I felt a tone of "don't ask again."

Research respondents felt the question of safety was a significant problem. Some suggested that if a sexual assault was experienced by a female salesperson after hours while being engaged at work, the police would request the company policy regarding employees working after business hours. The absence of such a policy is common, and I am still trying to secure such a policy within our medical industry.

An example of policy change occurs in the real estate industry, where it is normal practice for a female agent to be accompanied by another agent for after-hours appointments. These changes came about after several well-publicized appointment assaults in the last few years. If real estate agents can pull it together and look after their sales agents, why are we lagging so far behind in formulating an effective employee safety policy to protect hardworking salespeople?[4]

This important article highlights the following health and safety issues for salespeople in the United Kingdom; we still have the same issues.[4]

Other Areas of Sales Employee Safety

Driving

There is compelling evidence that company car drivers are at increased risk of accidents compared with the general population. One study found company car drivers to be 49 percent more likely to be involved in an accident. The reasons for the high accident rate among company drivers are varied. Research undertaken by *Adams-Guppy and Guppy* indicated that it was due to strong demands on time, which ultimately affected decision making regarding speeding and overtaking.[5]

Falling Asleep or Driver Fatigue

This accounts for a considerable proportion of accidents under monotonous driving conditions; circadian factors are as important in determining

---

[4]G. Harris, G. Mayho, and L. Page. 2003. "Occupational Health Issues Affecting the Pharmaceutical Sales Force." *Occupational Medicine* 53, pp. 378–83. doi:10.1093/occmed/kqg118.

[5]Adams-Guppy.

driver sleepiness, as is the duration of the journey. This identified the sales force as a "high-risk" group for road accidents and advised on the benefits to be gained from the introduction of clear policies to ensure that these individuals are protected.

Road Safety

There is a need to motivate employers to introduce road safety policies that reduce accidents and associated losses. Procedures should be employed to address work-related road safety, including risk assessment, driver training, incident reporting, mobile phone use, vehicle maintenance, ergonomics, breakdown guidance/assistance and alternative means of transport, incentive programs, and awareness campaigns.

Driver Safety Driving Courses

Undoubtedly, your company should enroll you in a driver defensive safety course. This covers car safety, braking, steering, and accident avoidance skills. Companies that do not support this essential training are lacking in care.

Violence

In 1999, there were an estimated 1.3 million incidents of violence at work in England and Wales, comprising six hundred and thirty-four thousand physical assaults and similar threats of violence. Occupations with above-average risks of violence were identified, and although the sales force does not, as a group, fall into a "high-risk" category, when compared with the national average, the report finds that employees who work in the evenings are at greater risk of violence at work and feel more exposed to threat and harassment.

Mobile Phone Use

Analysis of scientific studies on the hazard potential of mobile phones when used in vehicles unequivocally shows a marked impairment of driver performance. The evidence reveals that the use of mobile phones while driving has a detrimental effect on the driver's reaction time. Bluetooth has now avoided such infringements when driving. The purchase of a Bluetooth device is cheap and helps avoid losing your license for a period of time.

Drugs

Employers should be encouraged to have a clear policy on drugs and alcohol. This policy should actively discourage all employees from using such substances during working hours or when driving on business. The sales force is a group that may be placed in a difficult position, as the role includes organizing and participating in late meetings and conferences. During the Australian research interview process, some salespeople confirmed their company had encouraged or installed a mandatory drug test process.

In some countries, professions such as truck driving, ambulance driving, flying, and many others require a drug test on a regular basis.

Ergonomic Issues

The most important factor in reducing the risk of low back pain due to long driving or lifting is the implementation of a robust manual handling policy for employees, combined with a risk assessment and management approach involving line managers and employees. Sorry to be cynical about this point, but good luck with this one.

Holiday Work Contact

Holiday work contact is now becoming a big issue in sales. By force of habit, salespeople scan their phone regularly during holidays for any e-mails or orders, reply to customers and managers, and take calls. One solution to the problem is to have two mobile phones—one for work and the other for time off.

Healthy Eating

I was very surprised to be cornered in the office one day by our human resources assistant, who asked, "What time do you have lunch and for how long?" I felt the question did not even warrant an answer, but I answered her question, saying, "Perhaps never." Changing your diet dramatically for a period of time is not good, and doing this on a regular basis can't help.

Skin Cancer Safety as a Driver

As professional drivers, we do forget the care of our hand/arm skin in the car. Global companies do not present this and the dangers of skin cancer as a problem to their outside employees. Only recently, I had a squamous cell cancer removed from my left hand, presumably developed over many years of driving and sun exposure during driving.

Employees can help minimize ultraviolet (UV) exposure when driving, and this may include:

Reducing the amount of time in the car on high UV days. A company providing skin protection (50 UV Plus) for use in your car and covering doctor visits for mole map tracking. In Australia and the United States, where sun exposure is a problem, it should be made mandatory for companies as a safety precaution of high importance.

In addition, eye care is important. In the short term, exposure to high doses of UV radiation can cause certain eye conditions, some of the more serious long-term problems being:

Cataracts, retina damage to the cornea, overgrowth of the conjunctiva, and cancers of the conjunctiva. Symptoms to watch out for are gritty eyes, difficulty looking at light, swelling in the eyes, and blurred vision.

While not suggesting that the company provide sunglasses for driving, we believe you should spend a reasonable amount on a good pair of ultraviolet driving glasses to protect your eyes. Put on your sunglasses every time your drive, even if it is overcast!

Headspace When Driving

Going back to issues such as burnout and work stress, these and other intrinsic and external pressures greatly influence how you drive and function behind the wheel. Including drinking and taking drugs. Before turning the key, stop to think: "Am I in a clear state of mind to drive?"

Here are some personal accounts of risk and safety I have experienced.

Account A—Injury at Work

In my last year as an account manager, I was packing an urgently needed product to deliver to a customer. Rushing to tape up the box, I cut myself deeply in my left hand. Running around the office to seek assistance, I was told by the office staff that the first aid kit was to be found in the customer service center. Running to the customer service office and sitting down for assistance, I was looked at with horror by the staff. Asking where the first aid kit was, and bleeding all over their lovely clean desk, I found out there was no first aid kit. I then decided to take myself to hospital, where I had seven stitches.

I did not receive calls from any manager as to how I was, but I received an e-mail the next day from human resources, requesting me to attend a meeting at 9 a.m. The meeting was not about the company's concern that I had a serious accident and had lost all feeling in my left finger but about a complaint from the customer service staff about my verbal frustration and why I was in their office bleeding on their precious desk. I did point out to the human resources representatives that I was the victim and that I thought the accusation against me was unreasonable. Nothing I said would make them budge. I was dumbfounded at this situation and, furthermore, was requested to apologize in writing to the customer service staff that very day.

This illustrates issues with the rights of victims and the rights of the accuser. The company had failed to alert staff that they had a very good first aid room available in the warehouse. Embarrassment ensued among the staff, and my rights were eventually upheld when I was offered a royal tour of the first aid room. This did indicate that the company realized I was the victim; however, at no time did they apologize for their behavior.

Account B—Detained in Bali

During my tenure as sales manager for Southeast Asia, I was somewhat new to the international markets and unfamiliar with individual country laws. My boss was everything to me, and I trusted him implicitly. He was the best salesperson I have ever been mentored by, and I emulated his style and selling techniques to a T. My business area of responsibility was Singapore, Indonesia, Hong Kong, New Zealand, and the Philippines. I received a fax from a doctor in Semarang, Indonesia, requesting my assistance in a device procedure the following month. Picking up the products at head office in Sydney, I discussed the requirements of the procedure with my boss and caught the flight out the next day to Denpasar.

Arriving in Denpasar the following morning, I checked through customs, unaware of the attention I was receiving. Just as I was near to the green line to exit, I was detained by two customs officers and told I was cautioned for smuggling medical devices into Indonesia without local statutory approval. I was amazed that this could happen to me and was escorted to an interview room adjacent to the customs department. I waited about 3 hours in the heat to be interviewed by a senior customs officer. He went on to interrogate me for some time. He had my bags opened and was showing the sterile devices packed within. I explained the products were samples and that I was showing them to a doctor in Semarang the following day. This went on for what I thought was hours, and during this time his assistant was continually hitting his back pocket, signifying "you pay money now." I was smart enough to resist his persistent invitations, and, finally, the lights came on.

I reached into my notes and pulled out a business card of the doctor I was to work with, a Colonel in the Indonesian Army.

In Indonesia, nobody argues with a military Colonel!

Quickly, I was offered apologies and sent on my way to the flight that had left hours before for Semarang. Eventually, I arrived back in Sydney to meet up with my boss, who knew all the details. To my surprise, he said, "Well, that was a close one, ah?" Nothing more.

These two stories are true and demonstrate the lack of care and safety provided by companies to their people in the field. Call it what you will, but intentionally placing me in a very compromising position overseas was irresponsible and careless. When I arrived home, there was nothing said by human resources about my situation overseas; in fact, I would go so far as to say that they were probably not told.

Speaking with other colleagues today, I have learnt that not a lot has changed regarding safety for salespeople traveling overseas.[6]

Excessive working hours and how to manage time.
What are excessive working hours in sales today? Many global companies want their sales staff on territory no later than 8 a.m. This is fine, but one has to begin much earlier in order to be, for example, in an operating theater at, say, 7 a.m.

Pharmaceutical salespeople do start later, as seeing doctors is difficult before 10 a.m. The general working hours other than in the pharmaceutical sector is about 10 hours per day, 5 days per week. This equates to a 60- or 70-hour week all up. Working in the Asia Pacific, we worked 6 days per week, having Sundays off.

Europe's Ban on 50-Hour Weeks

In other Western countries, the facts don't bear this out. In six of the top 10 most competitive countries in the world (Sweden, Finland, Germany, Netherlands, Denmark, and the United Kingdom), it's illegal to demand more than a 40-hour work week. You simply don't observe the 70-hour work weeks that have become the norm in some parts of the United States, Australia, and New Zealand.

Sweden has led the Scandinavian countries with its renowned family-friendly policies by shifting to a **6.5 hour sales day**. Businesses across the Scandinavian countries are implementing the change so workers can spend more time at home or doing the activities they enjoy; this has also extended to sales in selected sectors.

Many would argue further that a shorter working sales week would inevitably affect overall sales results. The evidence says otherwise.

Work–life balance is now an international workplace issue. Within Scandinavia, the sales profession also follows the law (or do the sales people bend the law?), When we turn to hours worked in sales per week, we see the average as follows.

---

[6]Personal account Eden White.

What are the standard working hours in sales? In Australia, thirty-eight hours per week is statutory legislation and listed on your employment contract, but we all know, especially if you are new in the job, that you will put in excessive hours to become established. After a few years in the position, you will still be working the same 60 hours per week or have pegged back for a more realistic working week.

LinkedIn reports roughly three hundred thousand salespeople and account executives currently in the workforce. This suggests 300,000 * 70 = 21 million salespeople hours is being worked in the world today.

In the United States, the researchers discovered that sales reps work an average of 50 hours per week. Of those hours, they spend only 22 percent of their time selling and actively seeking out new business.

In the United Kingdom, research shows that working hours vary according to the sector but are generally quite long and can exceed 50 hours per week.

While it may look like we are working longer hours than are other countries, the average actual number of hours worked in sales has decreased in the last few years, according to the Australian Bureau of Statistics.

This is a generalization of "sales," not specifically medical sales. Most sales reps will tell you they use their time efficiently. Unfortunately, this is an exaggeration of the sales industry and could be verified only by a time clock measuring each day's work.

The goal is to be, as much as you can, face-to-face with your customer, conducting selling activities. The most surprising statistic is that we spend only about 10 to 15 percent of our day in front of the customer, while forfeiting 40 percent of our day conducting administration activities. If we introduce official shorter working hours, for example, no salesperson should work longer than a 35-hour week. Would we increase productivity and sales, or would we become less productive? The question here is, do we think 15 percent is enough face-to-face time in front of the customer to produce sales excellence? The answer here is no.

Apart from believing in yourself, one of the key sales drivers are "doing the numbers." This means seeing as many customers in your territory as possible. Of course, quality sales calls are a priority, but seeing the numbers of customers will clock up a far greater funnel list of opportunities than a sales person that is seeing only, say, two customers per day. The pharmaceutical industry has gone as far as stipulating a specific number of doctors to see per day. How does this equate to fewer hours per week? It clearly doesn't and will create a heaver workload.

I would go so far as to say that if a company mandates meeting a specific number of sales calls per day, this will be abused and may cause fudging of sales call numbers. Alternatively, if a sales rep is not aware of the company sales call benchmark per day, then this could create fewer customer calls than desired.

The following table tells us what we do with our average selling day.

- Entertainment   4 percent
- Face-to-face meetings   10 percent
- Mobile/telephone   10 percent
- Eating   3 percent
- Account planning funnel creation   2 percent
- Customer issue resolution   5 percent
- Business development in territory   1 percent
- Expense reporting   5 percent
- Internal processing   25 percent
- Sales meetings   8 percent
- Company meetings   2 percent
- Training/sales & product   3 percent
- Travel time   12 percent
- Waiting to see customer   6 percent
- Communications   4 percent

Anecdotal information compiled from several companies based on the medical industry 2018. No research has been documented on this statistic.

Top Performers and How They Use Their Hours in a Day

The standout differences on the preceding chart shows that top performers spend 8 percent on entertainment and 10 to 20 percent on face-to-face meetings.

Where top performers are different in their use of time, they increase face-to-face customer contact to 20 percent increase telephone customer contact, and account planning. Leaders would like to see this and even a greater reduction of internal processing from 14 percent down to 10 percent.

So how does this correlate with the current scenario of excessive salesperson working hours? In general, we do not have a "Personal Planning Process."

This Was My Week's Planning Break-Up

The difference between the documented figures and my own lay in face-to-face customer meetings, where I would spend up to 30 percent of my time.

Where Can You Trim Wasted Hours Further?

Reduce entertainment, customer resolution, expense, and internal processing time, allowing you to increase your customer face-to-face and telephone contact. It is not all that hard, requiring only some simple changes to your daily habits and follow-through with a small degree of "discipline" to increase face-to-face meetings. By the way, do not do your company expenses at work.

Simple Changing to Your Outlook Diary Habits Can Give More Time

During my coaching career, filling in time around sales calls was, I believe, the biggest time-wasting problem and undue procrastination, customer relationship management (CRM) information overload, the boss wanting useless reports on a priority basis, personal calls, and poor management of time allotted to the day's activities.

We all do this but tend to be less aware of how much time is actually being wasted. If we addressed this problem carefully and systematically, reduced time wasting and redeployed it into face-to-face customer engagement, sales would increase exponentially overnight.

Discipline—Who Is the Master?

The fundamental attribute all salespeople share is individual self-discipline. It is this that allows them to keep the commitments that they make to themselves. They know that exercising self-discipline will get the job done eventually. You've heard it before, but it bears repeating: successful people do what unsuccessful people aren't willing to do. It's not that the unsuccessful are unable but that they are unwilling.

The following six areas require a thoughtful, disciplined approach

1. **The discipline of prospecting:** There is one area of sales where self-discipline makes a tremendous difference and is rarely found. That area is prospecting. You can immediately produce better sales results by applying your self-discipline to prospecting. Salespeople with no real sales abilities or skills often outperform those with greater skills or abilities simply through disciplined prospecting. Go through potential clients in CRM one by one in a methodical manner, and the possibilities appear out of nowhere.

2. **The discipline of nurturing dream customers:** Your dream clients already have a supplier, maybe even a partner. Ignoring and neglecting your dream clients doesn't do anything to move you closer to the relationships that you need. The discipline of nurturing is what eventually opens the relationships that open opportunities. Your effort to create value for your dream clients before claiming any is what will eventually bear fruit.

3. **The discipline of following up:** Your clients and dream clients are judging you. They are watching to see if you keep your commitments. The discipline of following up is more than just sending the e-mail you promised to send. It's also the discipline of doing high-quality follow-up work. You make it easier for your customer to say yes when you observe the discipline of follow-up, keeping your word, and doing quality work.

    Practice the discipline of follow-up, and be someone who can always be counted on. You are ultimately judged by your customer if you keep promises. I found keeping my promise is paramount to success for sales.

4. **The discipline of continuous improvement:** You can't afford to rest on your laurels. Although you did the work to turn your dream customer into a paying customer, becoming complacent can cost you their business. From quarter to quarter, you have to improve what you do for your customers. You have to share with them the value that you are creating, as well as your plans for creating even more value together in the future. Each sale brings value to your customer base; however, it also brings greater discipline and skill improvement to you too.

5. **The discipline of personal development:** The environment that we live and sell in is like nothing we've ever seen before. The forces of globalization make for some difficult selling. Success means that you have to become the very best possible sales version of yourself. You need to become version two. The self-discipline of personal development begins with your ability to identify and eliminate distractions and bad habits. Instead of filling in downtime with distractions and useless inactivity, you have to use some of that time to improve yourself through reading, studying new courses, taking a class, or attending sales webinars.

6. **Taking personal calls at work:** Taking mobile calls from friends, acquaintances, and family each day adds up. Five 4-minute calls per day by 5 days a week will clock up to well over an hour on the phone not working. I am not advising you to stop this activity completely. Rather, let your friends and family know that you are at work and that you will call back after 6 p.m. Tell them to text you instead or call after hours.

An example of this, working with a young sales rep for a training day and she received over 10 personal mobile calls. This said to me she was happy to take calls from her friends all day!

Working from Home or Your Car

When you see sales teammates only in a brief chat or a weekly video call, it's hard to develop the sales camaraderie that makes for truly great teams. Let's look at working from home in today's professional selling. Most global companies want you out of the office in front of the customers.

The transition to having us out of the office and mobile came around 30 years ago.

No longer did you have the importance of your own desk and items that stayed where they were left. This transition was driven by two theories: firstly, to push the salespeople out of the office on the assumption that this would generate greater interaction with customers; secondly, having individual state offices accommodating rep rooms was seen as extravagant. Cost of office space is at a premium, so in the end, management had to find an alternative working environment, and hence the car or home office.

The next step was a total ban on working in the office, with management making it clear you were not welcome and ignoring the issue of where you could do your administration. The replacement office was the company car or home office.

Today's Sales Office

Companies want you to use your car or home for a number of reasons. Even at the interview stage, it is made clear that the sales position functions are on the road. Working from the car or home is the norm now; however, companies turn a blind eye to the problems involved in working remotely.

Face-to-Face Interaction Has Now Been Lost

One of the issues that I have encountered working remotely is differences that arise from different cultural expectations and work ethics. There is a temptation to take a few hours here or there. Activities such as doing the washing, preparing a meal for the night, or popping out for some shopping creep in and set up a habitual problem. Many would argue with me on this point, saying, "I have a disciplined routine and never stray from work at home" or "this is one of the 'perks of the job.'" Surprisingly, many sales reps believe that taking time off here and there is owed to them because they justify working long hours.

Everybody that has worked from home at some time has broken the rules. But, then, what are the rules?

Working independently with just a computer screen to keep you company is vastly different from the hustle and bustle of an office. Then, again, many would argue that the quietness of home as a place to work is better and that it is more productive than the office environment. After taking into account the downside of working from a car or home, I believe the upside is superior. In the end, I got greater productivity as the office distractions were not there. Many of my sales colleagues also argue that the office is too distracting and that they would prefer to work from home.

Control of Data and Information

Remote workers must balance various, almost overwhelming, communication streams. There are instant messaging apps, video call software, project management tools, and, of course, the ever-present e-mail coming through on your mobile phone. With so many channels to check, managers are, understandably, worried about information slipping through the cracks. One fortunate benefit of working for larger companies is that they have very good control of information via Virtual Private Network (VPN).

Low Reliability and Retention

Remote workers tend to look at jobs as a stepping stone or waypoint in the transition to something bigger and better. And since the team spirit is harder to develop among remote workers, they feel no guilt about moving on to new opportunities. However, trust can be an issue, unless it's an employee who relocated. Some remote workers like this style of work as they can hide away, thinking they are not above water to be noticed. This is a falsehood.

Reliability is a problem for most interstate teams, but when you remove the manager's presence, things can turn catastrophic. And even after you've taken the time to train remote workers so they are effective, what happens if they just stop answering your e-mails and disappear without a trace? An example of this was a sales person that went overseas for a holiday and never returned. Apparently, she met a partner and did not contact the company about her proposed return. The company resorted to having some of her colleagues make personal contact with her, and eventually she did return some weeks later to face the music.

In some companies contending with global time differences are enormous. This problem exists in the United States and Australia, with time gaps of up to 3 to 4 hours behind.

This places an extra burden on sales managers, requiring them to organize their time more into territorial blocks. Sales managers get this, but the temptation to call a distant sales member at 7 p.m. their time is always happening. This raises the question, do you turn your phone off at 6 p.m. or answer the call?

Remote work is a skill you should be adding to your résumés by documenting past experiences. Speak to people who have done it before or who have run their own businesses. These are great indicators of initiative and independence.

When considering working for a company that has a head office in another state, consider the following communications issues: What are the company's expectations of contact each day, and are you required to take early morning calls from head office? Are you required to attend sales meetings online early in the mornings, and are you given time to respond to requests from sales managers coming through late in the day?

Think through the remote selling issues, and be completely aware of the pitfalls before proceeding.

Loss of Productivity

Most remote sales members become comfortable with working from home, car, or hotel and need little to no insight as to what they are doing during the day or how distracted they may be. This is fine for self-starters and responsible employees but not so great for junior and/or unproven sales teammates.

Working from Coffee Shops

Background noise, massive distractions, unreliable Internet access due to a poorly maintained connection and/or capacity and overuse issues, and annoying shop neighbors are just some of the distractions you have to put up with. Remote doesn't work for some salespeople. It works for those who are self-reliant and can manage themselves alone. Again, discipline is the key to this type of sales position.

Suggestion

Stick to an objective and use a plan for the day. Keep to the plan and don't deviate. I am not saying, "Don't put the washing on," but do this early and hunker down for the day's work as if you were in a working environment. Have a workplace away from TV, and perhaps have a workplace devoid of any personal distractions. Perhaps make up your office devoid of pictures and personalization.

Security Issues to Consider

For remote sales workers and businesses that may employ them, the loss of a laptop or phone is catastrophic. A few years ago, I had a nightmare about someone stealing my laptop, I would have woken up in a cold sweat, screaming loud enough to wake up my family. Now, with the ability to host so much online and protect your data, I would probably just wake up and triple-check if my laptop was still there. However, this is a very real concern, especially if your business deals with sensitive data.

Precautions for Tech Devices at Work (Mobile Phone, Laptop, Tablet, etc.)

- Use VPN always.
- Upgrade your pin every 2 to 3 months.
- Be alert to physical threats such as theft of computer or mobile phone from your vehicle.
- Loss of mobile phone or computer devices at home office.
- Avoid such devices on display in your car or home, and utilize a door lock in the office.
- Disallow your family members access to such work devices.

- Ring-fence sensitive data in your data center so only thin client access is allowed.
- When traveling, do not let your devices out of your sight.
- Using e-mail for private use is treacherous—use private e-mail from another device.

Conclusion

When management decided to push us out of the office to work remotely, many years ago, they didn't realize the overall benefits to salespeople. Now, we have communication aids at our fingertips, with the protection of VPNs and the cloud. However, if you work remotely, you need to be mentally equipped and disciplined. Don't kid yourself—I mean disciplined!

I found it liberating and was far more productive.

CHAPTER 6

Are We Expendable in Selling Today and what value you bring to the company?

What of the Future?

This chapter discusses the evolution of professional salespeople and the value they bring to selling in the modern age.

Sales in general has changed over the last few years. Salespeople can't afford to be pushy, deceiving, lying, or any of those other nasty words. *Buyers hold the power now.* I am not drawing a line between professional salespeople and door–to-door salespeople, but today's professional has evolved away from this older style into a more sophisticated salesperson.

According to research from Forrester, one of the most influential research and advisory firms in the world, "over 1 million salespeople in America will be obsolete by 2020."[1] In fact, only one of the four salesperson types will survive the digital shift that we're experiencing.

B2B and B2C Selling Types—What Is B2B Sales Experience?

A sales candidate was searching for a sales job and came across some sales job postings that required **B2B** sales experience. What is B2B, and how do you go about getting it? B2B is an acronym for **business to business** and in this case relates to **business to business sales.**

---

[1] Forrester United States.

What's the Difference?

B2B sales differs from **B2C, or Business to Consumer.** Both these descriptions are generic and pertain not only to the medical sales area but also to general sales. The main difference is the target audience for products or services. The call points are different, and the sales approach is different for each target. For example, a B2B (business 2 business), sales professional selling to a business will need to get past a gatekeeper and find the decision maker, which is typical of capital hospital sales. A B2B sales rep will need to identify the person with the buying power within an organization and get in front of him or her to sell their product or service. Selling directly to the consumer requires dealing with different buying cycles, and the decision-making process will be different.

A B2B sales professional might sell professional services such as health care, software, support, or consulting to other businesses. Selling in the B2B market space is different than in B2C (business 2 customer), but there are also selling skills that apply to both, so if you don't have specific B2B sales skills, don't count yourself out just yet. It is your job to identify the skills you have to match the needs of the hiring company.

Why Would a Company Request B2B Experience?

Any job opening requires the best candidate with certain skills and experience to hit the ground running and to bring results fast. The sales manager will not have to train a person with previous B2B sales experience on how to sell the product or service. So not all sales experience is the same, and for higher-priced or more technical products such as software, experience goes a long way.

Distributor to Customer Selling

This is another skill to demonstrate. What is different is that you are not selling for a principal manufacturer or global organization; you represent a product or group of products that is an agency for a manufacturer locally or overseas.

Selling under such circumstances is very different than in the case of the preceding styles. The product description and function are dictated by another company you indirectly represent while working for your distributor company as your direct employer.

Currently, Salespeople Fall into the Following Styles of Selling

An analysis of the main types of sales styles shows that we all generally fall into the following styles or a combination of several styles. *Which one are you?*

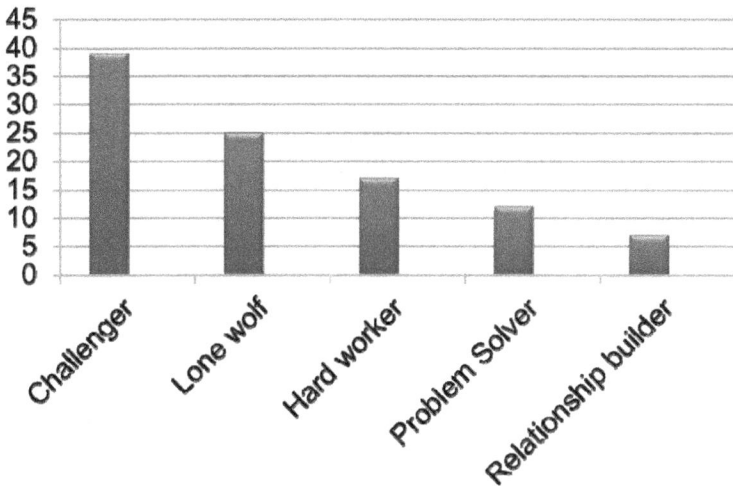

Figure 6.1 Various modes of customer buying

Who Is the Best Seller?

The best salesperson in this chart is said to be the challenger. He or she challenges the customer carefully, but the customer appreciates the counsel offered. The person who says, "I am a relationship builder first" is, unfortunately, not selling actively, being more concerned with building relationships and hoping sales will fall into his or her hands. The lone wolf can be a good sales person but wants management to leave him or her alone. Unfortunately, such salespersons are not team players and are seen as an outdated or dinosaur salespersons today.

It is helpful to incorporate traits from each of these types into your selling style, as, ultimately, there is not one that is the best or a combination of the best. I firmly believe that we all have a percentage of all of them but at varying levels to make up one rounded sales person. However, the challenger is always found to be the best and most successful seller.

So, to bring together our sales patterns of behavior and meet the future on how we seek information, are we heading in the right direction for the next 10 years? Where do we need to change, or should we just let things evolve naturally?

The overall driving force is what the customer needs. We can change our style, selling behavior, and many other facets of our sales persona, but, ultimately, the customer will drive the sellers out and into the field.

Consumer Buying Habits Today

The following graph shows lifestyle and business modes of buying, presented by HubSpot consumer behavior survey in 2016.

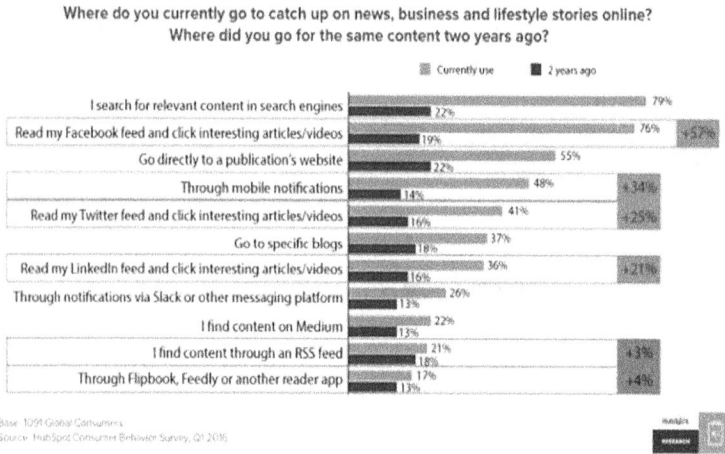

Figure 6.2 Consumer buyer behavior survey

Source: © HubSpot Consumer Behavior Survey 2016

As recently as 2016/2017 and 2018, this research showed a dramatic change in buyer methods of seeking information. We instinctively Google the product or service we need as a first move.

Studying global consumer trends clearly reveals that consumers want visual information, interesting articles to read, online education, and interactive visual stimulus. Interestingly, in the Australian research, all interviewees overwhelmingly replied that professional salespeople will be selling in similar positions within 10 years, citing the need for customer contact to engage the sale.

Traditional Sales Tactics Are Said to Be Outdated

Sales training companies, which are selling updated sales courses today, are inventing new and supposedly innovative ways to meet the new demands of sales. When you dig deeper into the content of these new sales training courses, you find the basics to be the same seven steps of the sale or a select part of the seven steps.

Pharmaceutical and medical device sales representatives face mounting challenges earning the all-important face time with health care buyers. Everyone is short on time, and no one wants to spend valuable minutes listening to a sales pitch for a product they're not even sure they need.

Sales professionals have to work even harder to stand out of the crowd and capture the attention of their target prospects. On the other hand, going too hard will bring you down so fast that your customer base will not want to see you any further.

Buyers Want to Decide, Rather Than Be Sold Too; Is This True?

Today, the buyer is far better informed even before they see a sales person. Sales organizations that take a consultative approach provide their prospects with educational content that aids buying decisions, earning trust and establishing authority, which helps the company secure the sale.

We Should Change Our Selling Behavior

We all have to take this seriously. I started working in 1974 and had to totally reinvent myself many times. Think about how to continually update your technological knowledge. If you aren't up on mobile tools, CRM (customer relationship management), and general technology trends, you may not even know what to sell and how to position it. Yes, we should continually be altering our skills and style to meet the market expectations today.

Read as Much as You Can

Today, tools like Twitter, Facebook, LinkedIn, and the web, in general, are rapidly becoming reading systems and industry forums for our customers. If you subscribe to the people and topics you like, you will start to see articles and news on your industry that will rapidly bring you "into the market" and help you see what is going on and what you need to learn.

In my estimate, within 10 years about 60 percent of the sales situations currently being handled by salespeople will be handled automatically; however, there will continue to be a need for salespeople in the following situations:

Situations Where the Customer Needs Assistance

The Customer Cannot Define a Solution

For example, a company might understand that it's experiencing manufacturing delays and know exactly where those delays are taking place but lack the expertise to change the process or technology in order to reduce or eliminate them. In this case, the customer will turn to a salesperson to define and propose a solution and perhaps come up with a product that may correct the problem. This is where the challenger could play a useful role as an advisor.

The Customer Cannot Calculate the Return on Investment (ROI)

For example, a company's executives may intuitively understand that purchasing a system to make manufacturing run more efficiently would be a wise investment but may still not be able to calculate whether the ROI of an in-house system would be greater than one that was outsourced. In this case, the customer will turn to a salesperson to help create a business case for purchasing the solution.

Salesperson to Customer

Although we can assume our customer has researched well prior to the sales call, we must not assume they have all the facts. Listening to the need first will give you a starting position for product placement. The customer may merely want to see the product so it matches the image they have in their own mind—the curiosity factor.

The customer will be, as now, entrusted with fully investigating several similar products and will need to feel, touch, and assess. A sales person will also need to survey or trial the product intention. Selling in the future will be specific in that the product must be exactly what the customer needs. There will be a firming up of relationships, including questioning such things as service, warranty, and costing in this mix.

Conclusion

Today, we're observing a rapid adoption of game-changing technologies like voice search and conversational UI (user interfaces). As big players like Google, Facebook, Amazon, Microsoft, and even Tesla, push their innovations forward, we're on the cusp of another major shift in consumer behavior. For businesses, many of these new technologies and resulting behaviors that they will create will bring about even more channels for their products to be discovered by consumers.

Conversational interface is any user interfaces (UI) that mimics chatting with a real human. The idea here is that instead of communicating with a computer on its own inhuman terms by clicking on icons and entering syntax-specific commands, you interact with it on yours, by just telling it what to do. The use of UI now is so integrated into sales and customer interaction that it has the potential to take over the primary investigative phase of buying.

From the Management Point of View

Executives struggle with how salespeople should add value, especially in today's multichannel environment, along with marketing being pulled into the sales combination.

Greater professionalization is needed in countries where the state of the profession is less developed. Emergent strategy is practiced, though not universally. Sales executives generally believe that little incremental value in technology can be gained, though it is apparent that technology is not being fully utilized. Technology is racing very fast for us. Are we keeping up?

Does the customer want interaction, and at what stage of the sale process? How do we gauge when to come in and when to leave? Training on this very important subject is imperative. No sales training I have seen incorporates this, but I believe this is the key to customer interaction in the future.

When we go back to the "great divide" subject, this exemplifies the problem between sales, sales management, and marketing having a go at what type of UI promotion should be opened.

So, Are Sales Professionals Expendable in the Future?

The answer is, possibly "yes" because there is an element of unknown in how general professional sales is moving. Alternatively, I firmly believe that the customer, in general, wants point of sale to customer interaction, especially if the sale is high in cost and there are mutable key decision makers.

So, do we feel we are becoming obsolete yet? Yes and no. If we continue to multiply our way of engaging the customer on a more helpful and realistic basis, I think we will still be doing the same but slightly different in our job function for decades to come. That's the good news.

Technology and the Implications for Us as Salespeople

Major global companies provide us with VPN (virtual private network), mobile communications, and selling aids within these devices we carry around. Communication to customers now is immediate, and this is the customer expectation. Product information, quotes, and other information are able to be sent on the run. No longer do we need to have marketing personnel send out this information if it is at the salespersons' fingertips.

So, what are the implications for our health, family life, and work processes, and does technology assist us to get the business in the end? The overriding technology (software) is CRM, Oracle, Net Suite, Pipedrive, and Sales Force, which are just some of the software offerings utilized out there.

The Positives and Downsides to Customer Relationship Management Software (CRM)

Missing Key Information

CRM data often contains gaps in information. Relying on basic demographic data or purchase history is no longer sufficient. Supplement basic information with more detailed information, such as purchasing preferences or web history. Without this type of information, it's difficult to understand how to reach customers effectively.

The positives are varied and comprehensive. Starting a new job with your entire customer base recorded and a list of the past customer interactions is wonderful. In a way, just pick up from the last representative and start sales calls. I am told new editions of CRM are addressing these issues. One word of warning: When starting, do not spend too much time on the CRM data; do it quickly and get out there selling.

Out-of-Date Information

Customer information changes often, but the data that marketers mostly use to reach customers doesn't always update as quickly as we'd like. Whether a consumer has moved to a new city or has changed his or her purchasing habits, campaigns will not be effective if marketers are relying on information that does not update as customers change their jobs and move on.

Incorrect or Unverified Data

Similarly, the data used for marketing campaigns needs to be accurate from the start. Marketers often rely on unverified data that could be incorrect. For marketing campaigns to be effective, it is crucial for marketers to reach consumers in a highly targeted way. Without verifying information, marketing efforts and resources could be wasted.

Lack of Insight

Even if CRM data is up to date and accurate, it's still just data. It provides marketers with as much information as possible about a customer but doesn't reach conclusions. Marketers need to use this information to uncover their own insights to effectively reach consumers at the right time, through the right channel and with the right message. The marketing department should utilize the contacts area to further update customers with new products that are related to each specific sales group.

Inability to Find New Prospects

While CRM data can be useful for reaching current customers, it does not help sales reach new customers. It's important for marketers to effectively reach consumers who have the potential to become loyal, long-term customers.

Privacy Concerns

CRM databases are not responsive to the challenges of multichannel marketing in an increasingly privacy-protected society. It is important for marketers to identify and contact clients and prospects according to their unique privacy requirements.

CRM data can be very useful and often leads to highly successful campaigns. But marketers need to keep these potential issues in mind before relying on this information. Overlooking these common problems leads to incomplete or inaccurate profiles of your customers and can lead companies down the wrong path.

Using CRM on the Mobile

My 10 consecutive years using CRM were great, and I won a national award for its use. My constant complaint to management was that CRM was unable to update a sale call on your mobile; I hope the new version of CRM has solved this.

Overall, CRM has been a great technical introduction and aid to salespeople, not forgetting its usefulness to management. We have long felt the critical need to save time in our sales job, and CRM provides the answer to this vexatious problem.

I loved using CRM, which has proved to be a great product, as with many other similar kinds of software.

Note: Permission given to author to use CRM product as reference from Darshi McKenzie Microsoft Dynamics 2017.

1. **CRM growth not slowing down:** According to a forecast, the CRM market will be worth $37 billion in 2017. Since 2011, each year around 70 percent of businesses have consistently stated that they plan to increase spending on technology such as this.

   Years ago, salespeople resisted CRM, but embracing such technology now is imperative, and most professional salespeople currently accept a form of CRM and utilize the benefits accordingly. When using CRM software to collect customer information, e-mail addresses, private and work contact numbers, and notes regarding meetings, ensure that customers have been asked for their permission in writing. I would suggest that many customers may not have given permission to use their sensitive information. Good business practice makes it both vital and ethical to have the customer's permission.

2. **Temptations:** In the early days of CRM, you would finish up around 3 p.m. in the field, not see any further customers, and fill in the day's activities. Filling in data for CRM information about the previous or full day's activity is essential, but the question is, when do I do this task? The new features added to CRM give you the opportunity to update information on your tablet or mobile, which is a huge time-saving advantage.

3. **Sales force automation systems:** Businesses without automation spend 71 percent of their time and resources planning and defining business processes. Selling requires a number of tedious, time-consuming, and repetitive tasks, such as scheduling sales appointments, sending follow-up e-mails, and updating sales opportunities, all of which reduce productivity and profitability.

4. **Sales force automation** (SFA) technology solutions automate many tasks, freeing up sales employees to focus on activities that generate more sales and revenue. SFA allows sales managers to keep their teams up to date on current and new products and services. With SFA, managers can also have instant access to activities of individual sales employees, sales figures, opportunities, customer complaints,

and other data used to determine sales success. Armed with information provided in real time, managers can take action and make adjustments quickly to optimize efforts.

5. **Mobile technology:** The proliferation of mobile devices, such as smartphones and tablets, has changed many aspects of the selling process forever. For customers, the ability to research, evaluate, and purchase products and services online using this technology has transformed the buying experience. Sales teams should take this into account.[2]

---

[2]Executives' perspectives of the changing role of the sales profession: views from France, the United States, and Mexico. The customer relationship management (CRM) market will be worth $37 billion in 2017. CRN and a clear explanation of the new way of customer recording software.

CHAPTER 7

The Big Divide Between Marketing and Sales

And How It Will Affect You in Sales?

This chapter discusses the practice that has become a divide between marketing, sales management, and sales team members. In past decades, this was practiced to engender respect for "upper and middle management." Unfortunately, this practice went on far too long. We should also cover at length on the way salespeople should be treated and respected.

Why Sales and Marketing Don't Get Along?

Sales and marketing teams pursue a common objective, create customer value, and drive company growth and results. But sales and marketing don't always get along. Some tension between sales and marketing is healthy and productive, but when they pull in different directions, the productivity decreases rapidly.

The Divide, Unfortunately, Remains Today

When a sales person is elevated to sales management to lead a team, the new sales manager goes through several changes. First, the feeling of importance hits them, then the sense of responsibility of the job, and, finally, "I now have to manage people that I know well and in some cases are friends." This is only one of the many scenarios that management faces when attempting to close the gap between management and sales members.

When I say a divide or gap between sales staff and marketing/sales management, for example, what am I saying?

For decades, there existed a love–hate relationship between marketing and sales. In the end, the game is to make sales profitably. Both departments must work together to create contact with a customer that needs a product or service. The strained relationship is not imaginary, but a real and tangible problem. Some would say it is better that the two departments work separately, but, in the end, both departments must reach the goal. **"Smarketing"** companies see a 27 percent faster profit growth and win 38 percent more deals if the relationship works harmoniously.

For example, a new marketing manager starts with the company and wishes to make his or her mark on the business. In doing so, there are casualties on the way, and an inevitable loss of communications begins.

According to the Aberdeen Group, an information technology research and analysis firm, organizations with optimized relationships between marketing and sales teams grow revenue up to 32 percent faster if marketing and sales work together well.

Perceived General Issues Seen Between Marketing and Sales

The following issues are a combination of problems that occur if marketing and sales are working in opposition rather than in sync.

- Sales funnel meetings are generally not combined and separated.
- Qualifying needs should be left to sales and marketing to help with sales progress.
- Passing on customer product trends is rare and not routinely practiced.
- Sales passing on new product development to marketing for R&D work.
- Common mapping of sales budget goals.
- How marketing can make it easier for information dissemination to the customer.
- Create a clear line of sales and marketing responsibility (identify a list of responsibilities).
- Marketing and sales not meeting to review what's on next.

Putting some or all of these issues together discloses a "screaming divide" between both departments. In some companies I have worked for, the divide has been enormous. The common reason behind this divide is predominantly power and personalities.

The Divide Grows Larger, or Can It Be Closed?

The gap between sales management and salespeople is worth the effort to consolidate.

An MBA (master of business administration), unfortunately, does not make you a leader of salespeople. The divide remains until the leader is prepared to do what he or she wishes the sales team to do. This is called leadership by example. Many leaders will not and do not endorse this leadership philosophy as they may feel it brings them down to the salesperson level. Many managers resist this proposal, but sales staff often say the boss is too far removed to be approached for help.

The time factor plays a critical role as many sales leaders are responsible for more than 10 sales staff, perhaps stretched over several states. They may desire to be better leaders but find it hard to find the time to practice their management skills. A management course may help with this important issue; however, if the course is a top-down or a dictatorial style course, the new sales manager will be indoctrinated before he or she hits the desk.

Many sales staff will have the following mixed relationship with their sales manager

- Respected and highly looked up to by all sales team members
- Positive and respectful relationship with all team members
- Not liked but respected for their ability
- Admired and respected, has complete confidence in the sales team
- Considered insufficiently skilled to coach or teach the sales team
- Considered a liar and watched carefully by sales team
- Considered a manager who dodges the opportunity to pitch in and help the sales team
- Never available and considered a waste of time
- Always looked up to as a great mentor

These are just a few of the more common attitudes of sales team members toward their direct leader. The leader who develops honest respect, is a good and supportive coach, and is always willing to stand up for his team members, no matter what, will be ahead on points. The leader that deliberately places a divide between the team and him or herself will eventually lose team support. I call this leader

JUST A FOOL!

What Do We Need to Improve the Gap between Marketing and Sales Departments?

A good example of cohesion between marketing and sales shows a clear delineation understood by both departments "at all levels." Having an understanding of who does what and where the lines cross is imperative, and you will find plenty of great examples of cooperation and productive cohesion between the two departments.

- **Leave your ego at home**

  Leaving the ego at the door suggests that personal agendas can creep into the misalignment. When you have one department that wants a bigger voice and control over decisions, getting the two to work together is near impossible. When companies spend between 30 and 40 percent of revenue to run both departments, you would expect cooperation. It takes a strong company director to turn this ego competition around.

  I held a sales position when I witnessed the great divide between sales and marketing and the egos at play. The current managing director either thought it was healthy to let this play out or was ignorant to the destructive dynamics. In the end it was partly responsible for the company not reaching plan for many years.

- **The customer has been forgotten**

  Caught up in this divide, the customer, ultimately, is not consulted regarding his or her current needs. This, in turn, drives marketing in the wrong product direction; not having up-to-date product/customer needs are ignoring the intention of the two departments.

- **Reason for the rift: One of these things is not like the other**
  For those that are not fully in the know, such as a new sales person, marketing and sales could be seen as the same division. This leads to the dangerous notion that a great marketing team can possibly render a sales team redundant or vice versa. In this situation, each of the departments may have the misguided attitude of superiority over the other. In this instance, big egos control what is a struggling sales and marketing operation.

Where Does This Leave You as the Salesperson caught up in the mess

If you are experiencing the sales–marketing disconnects, the best thing to do is *stay out of the argument*. However, if you are convinced that the last sale you lost and had nursed for months was affected by a lack of marketing input, speak to your sales leader and voice your opinion loudly.

Don't take the rap for losing a great sale if you were let down by another group of people. When a big sale is lost because a department has not contributed as they should, you have a right to call out the people responsible. I would suggest an e-mail to all marketing and sales leadership members pointing out the deficiency of lackluster help that you believe lost the business. Sometimes, it is better to stand up and be counted.

Disconnect with Your Sales manager and How to Fix It

When I say "a disconnect" with your sales manager, I refer primarily to loss of respect. We can also say a loss of ability to communicate, in general, a resistance to asking for assistance, and a wondering how you can turn this situation around between you and your sales manager.

Example: A colleague of mine called me yesterday and said, "I have now lost respect for my sales manager." She left a large global company 12 months ago with the promise of advancement from clinical sales to marketing. In her new position, she has, over the 12 months, shown incredible sales results and has proven herself outstandingly. A new marketing position was advertised, and she was encouraged to apply for the new position, which she did; she interviewed several times and made a short-list marketing presentation.

Yesterday, she was informed that an outside person was chosen for the position, whom she knows well and has little respect for. Crippled and disillusioned, she called me for advice on what to do next. This scenario will apply to all people in selling some time during the course of a working career. She is completely disappointed as her manager encouraged her and said the company wanted to appoint from within and that she was the strongest contender.

Yes, there could be a lot more behind the scenes, but this scenario plays out every day, and sales managers have to manage the disappointed salesperson back on the road to being productive. The problem here is that making statements such as "you are the strongest internal contender for the position" is setting yourself up, as a sales manager, to lose your top salesperson.

When we review why there is a disconnect between salespeople and sales management, I must refer you back to chapters dealing with lies and deception. All salespeople may take a dislike to their sales manager; however, just because you don't like the way they comb their hair, that should not impair the positive working relationship that must be maintained. If, however, your trust, respect, or unhappiness in how you are treated affects your working relationship, then I believe the breakdown is inevitable. Salespeople are very quick to assess a person quickly, and first impressions of their boss can make or break the new job.

So if one looks at this example as a divide between leadership and sales team members, then we still have a long way to go. It seems that if mistakes are made by the leaders, we never pass on the lessons learned, and they should be logged and saved in the "great mistakes cloud in the sky."

Why do we continue to make mistakes given that history has taught us otherwise?[1]

---

[1]PM Posted by Stacy Bouchard ug 26, 2015 1:00:00 PM/Like many sales people, we feel and see a divide between management and salespeople. This paper brings clarity to the issue.

Some Helpful Hints on How to Get along with Your Sales manager.

Please note: If you have to work on many of the following ideas, then perhaps a weekly consult with your coach is in order.

- Be on time and be early too.
- Be willing to help your manager with things they need quickly.
- Document opportunities and keep them realistic and up to date.
- Always be happy if they want to work in the field with you, and embrace the assistance.
- Encourage your boss to meet your customers.
- If advice comes your way, accept it, and make the effort to alter behavior.
- Always be honest and open with your ideas and thoughts.
- Show you are dedicated to getting the sales.
- Show you are keen to further education.
- Keep your paperwork such as expenses completed and sent on time.
- If you aspire for advancement, consult your sales manager.
- Always ask for their opinion.
- Endeavor to be on sales budget plan.
- Always be coming up with solutions to better sales results.
- Don't take unnecessary days off for illness.

Many more items can be added to this list, but these are what sales managers appreciate from a good sales team member. They look for dedication, honesty, and hard work along with achievement. The remainder just falls into place.

Performance Reviews in Short

At your performance review, if your manager is an honest person, he or she will express happiness over certain things and mention anything not going to plan. This review is a time for you to consolidate the working relationship between you and your sales manager. For performance reviews, you are generally given a prereview personal assessment sheet for your self-performance and your bosses' performance and support. This gives you a perfect opportunity to say what you need and raise any issues between you and your manager. Often, this is documented and you're given a personal copy. Think carefully about raising any derogatory issues before they go on paper, even to the point of scaling back the harshness of the comment. Always express views positively.

Sales managers just want a happy and performing team and dislike disharmony and poor sales, as this is a direct reflection of their management skills. A tiff or two is normal, but when a team member becomes averse to their manager in the team, disharmony prevails further.

Conflict Resolution in the Sales Team

How Common Is Conflict in a Sales Team?

When do conflicts in a sales team relationship influence sales team performance, and what is the underlying process by which this occurs? Although there is burgeoning interest in sales research at the team level, very few empirical studies have shed light on sales team dynamics such as conflict and how they impact sales team performance. When conflict occurs in the team, the sales team destruction dynamic starts and generally witnesses members either leaving or taking sides.

My personal observation is that unmanaged sales team conflict causes declining sales along with general individual disharmony and aggravation. The worst disharmony will cause outright arguments and fighting.

What Are the Top Six Sources of Conflict in a Sales Team?

- Commission/bonus paid
- Sales budgets
- Cross-territory boundary encroachment without notice
- Overreaching our responsibility
- Difficult team member not performing his or her job
- Personal dislike between team members, and jealousy

Of the preceding six sources of conflict, which is healthy conflict and destructive conflict, the most difficult to deal with is jealousy and personal dislike, a problem that exists in many sales teams everywhere. Causes of discontent are typically routine, and all can be rectified by a good manager.

Personal Dislike between Sales Team Members Is One of the Common Problems We See

Personality clashes happen eventually in a new sales team. When you put together a group of Type A personalities and ask them to get along in a competitive arena, some issues will arise. Dislike between two or more members (especially if it is in a small team) could be happening without the knowledge of other team members. Eventually, you will see this as they snipe at each other or disagree without cause. If it is left to fester over several months, reversing the dislike between the warring members is nearly impossible. The sales manager must immediately practice appropriate management skills in conflict resolution.

I prefer to knock the issue on its head immediately by getting the two parties off-site to thrash it out together on their own. Future interactions must be monitored, and if the warring continues, you will have to intervene as soon as possible. Letting conflict fester is a monumental mistake. Sometimes, just getting both warring parties together will sort the issue out. It is up to the two parties to be adultlike and willing to work on the problem together.

An amicable working relationship, and, ideally friendly team relationship, and individual team cooperation is vital for the sales members overall successful result. Sometimes, it is better to swallow your pride and push on. Making a friend of your enemy is a good move.

If All Else Fails

From the leader's point of view, before handing over to HR, try one more meeting with the two warring parties and appealing to their better judgment. Explain that there are casualties in these situations and that both of them could lose their jobs. Also explain that you will not tolerate the destructive behavior any further. Seek a final agreement between the two parties that they will endeavor to settle their differences, and let them know the company will not tolerate any further disruption.

Would You Be Open to External Counseling or Mediation?

If, after this final attempt, the opportunity is not taken up and the behavior still continues with the other party, perhaps some outside counseling would be helpful.

When there is conflict in the team, you will see the following behavior.

- A team member who sits back and avoids putting in, one who says yes but never delivers, or who says, "The order is coming" but it never arrives
- A team member who is constantly leaving home late to work and who is always sick and looking for excuses
- A team member who always talks up what he or she does but doesn't have much to show, always sucks up to the boss, and who makes excuses all the time
- A sales person with a lack of appointments for the coming weeks and a team member who shows a constant dislike for another sales member and causes disruption

These are just a few signs to look out for. If you have a sales colleague who displays at least two of these traits, the team has a problem to fix. Very little is written or studied on this topic. A study of worth is the following by Provo UT in 2016, which pointed more toward speaking up in general[2].

In a study of 1,025 people, Provo found that an astounding 72 percent of respondents reported instances when they or others failed to speak up effectively when a peer did not pull his or her weight. Sixty-eight percent reported a failure to address disrespect, while 57 percent let peers slide

---

[2]Provo, UT—December 6, 2016.

when they skirted important workplace processes. According to the data, the majority of the workforce is guilty of similar conversation failures.

Our research respondents estimate their avoidance costs their organizations an average of $7,500 per conversation in lost time and resources.

The Final Word on Personal Conflict in the Sales Team

If you are caught up in conflict within your team, either through politics or maybe something you said, step back for the good of the team and yourself.

Simple Steps You Can Take to Settle Conflict

- Step back with no political involvement whatsoever.
- Do not get involved in the blame game.
- Avoid your sales manager's attempts to get you involved in the argument.
- Remain unbiased in regard to the two warring parties.
- Try not to let the disruption affect your abilities and sales results.
- Try counseling if needed, your company may offer this service.
- Resist the invitation to be involved in mediation unless you are personally involved.

Your best position is to remain anonymous and impartial. This may be difficult, but, believe me, getting involved in sales team arguments and disputes is destructive and may drag you into an indefensible position, with consequences for your career. Take care of your *Me* brand first!

Conflict over Compensation Payments

This is often seen as one of the most contentious issues in sales team conflict.

You have an impression or understanding of what you are about to earn as commissions/bonus each quarter or year. You have worked this out according to the job description of the company sales commission scheme payments document (that's if you understand the workings). You then receive the payment, and it is totally different from your expectations.

You may get this cold feeling of "have I made a grave mistake, or have I been taken for a ride?" You think about this for a moment or two, and then call a sales colleague to see how they went. Depending on their response, you start either to panic or decide to confront your sales manager. Often, this panic is compounded if you have ordered a new car or a family holiday based on your own predicted commission payment calculations.

There may be issues here of deceptive communication.

The First Thing to Do

- Review your commission pay policy and calculation method; ask for a new copy.
- Keep your own sales results to double-check on.
- Stay cool and do not jump the gun on this problem, but sleep on it.
- Conduct a sales review and apply the calculation method again; do this several times.
- Confirm the results on paper, and put them into a memo to your sales manager if they are incorrect.
- Set up a time with your sales manager to discuss your grievances and take evidence.
- If you are wrong, don't make the same mistake twice.
- If, however, the company is wrong, smile and keep an eye on the future payments.

If there is a genuine mistake, some companies tell you that the payment will be in the next commission payment time frame. Do not accept this, as the delay may not be legal and the tax will be built into the next payment.

However, if, for instance, you find out your company has tried to dupe you and avoid payments that are rightfully yours, then you have only a few choices available:

- Hold the line on what you believe is right; don't give up.
- Document everything in writing, and set up a file of documentation.

- Make sure you keep your original commission scheme offer document.
- Give the company the opportunity to explain their actions and how they will make good the right payment.
- If you feel there is no contrition and you are unable to work for such people then your pride and integrity are paramount, and working for a deceitful company in this situation would be intolerable. Companies that do this to salespeople will do it again and again.

What If I Don't Understand the Commission System and How It Works?

I myself worked for a global company that paid commission each quarter and yearly. This was fine, but no sales team member could explain how it worked. When various leaders in the company were asked to explain the calculation method, even the CEO didn't seem to understand. The only leader in the company who could explain the method of calculation was the national sales manager, and only after numerous challenges for him or her to explain. In the end, this ambiguous commission scheme continued, and no one knew how the payments were calculated. Later on, when I interviewed this leader for the research study, I pressed him to explain this to me; he maintains that there was no intent to deceive but acknowledged it was hard to calculate.

In this case, the scheme could have been simplified and explained to the sales team members to engender more trust in the organization.

What Are the Normal Compensation Schemes on Offer?

As you would imagine, there are numerous styles of compensation plans being offered in the corporate sales industry. The principle of compensation offers is to compensate you for working long hours and weekends and for sales excellence over and above that.

Most compensation plans begin with incentive payments for reaching 90 percent of sales and then escalate to 100 percent, with further payments for being over sales budget. The point where percentage compensation is paid under 100 percent of the plan differs from company to company. Some may pay 2 percent of overall sales made or a higher percentage. The idea here is to encourage you to drive sales but compensate you for just getting there and the effort put in. Note that many sales people get close to the sales plan and get upset if they don't receive some compensation. This is the reason for recognition. In addition, payments under full budget are intended to recognize effort under difficult market conditions and I personally support this option.

Commission Paid for Overbudget Sales

The majority of companies provide a payment system that is simple and easy to calculate. Paying a percentage over sales budget either once per year or four times per annum is normal. For example, if your quarterly sales plan is two hundred and fifty thousand dollars of sales and you reach 100 percent of sales and you are being offered say 1.25 percent for reaching budget, your compensation payment over sales budget for the year that you should earn is $2,750, or a quarterly amount of $937.50.[3]

In other compensation plans, paying only sales over sales budget, the scenario is vastly different. If you are offered 1.25 percent of "sales over plan" and you sell $50,000 over your quarterly budget, you are due $625.00 for the quarter less tax.

Other companies get a little more complicated with dicing up different products and giving more for new product emphasis and promoting lines for a year or a marketing period. These compensation plans are complicated and difficult to audit from the salesperson's point of view.

Ongoing criticisms of overly complicating the payment system are usually leveled directly at the national sales manager for altruistic reasons. Very few companies go out to intentionally confuse their sales reps but come up with such ridiculous systems that you need to be an accountant to work out the end result.

---

[3]Sales Commission Structures: Which Model Is Best for Reps? A good review of several different commission structures to look at for ideas and employment reference. The Disadvantages of Percentage-Based Sales Commission Plans/Arthur Luke Arthur. Are these commission issues causing you to lose reps/Kendra Lee Oct 2014.

The alternative question is this: Do compensation schemes motivate salespeople to work harder? In my opinion, no. Many salespeople I have talked with about their particular sales commission schemes say:

- Not generally interested.
- If I get commission, it is a bonus I don't expect.
- I have no interest in the commission payments; never think of it.
- I generally forget it and let the end of the quarter surprise me.
- I breathe every day for a great commission payment.
- I plan my purchases and holidays around my commission.
- If I miss out on commission, I am devastated.

I myself always forgot about the commission payments for one reason: They distract you away from the real game—selling.

In the end, a commission or bonus is what we call a "BONUS" meaning the sugar on the cake. Don't let yourself be engrossed in day to day thought about earning commission payment if you are on a good package.

Operational Budgeting Defined

For you to argue that your sales budget is a "big stretch," it is best to know how budgets are formed first. Budgeting is part of the management control process by which managers ensure that resources are obtained and used efficiently and effectively in the accomplishment of the organization's objectives. There are several kinds of budgets, and while specific terminology may vary from company to company, budgets generally fall into one of three categories.

1. **Capital budgets:** These budgets portray the corporation's planned and approved capital expenditures for periods of one to 10 years.
2. **Financial budgets:** Such budgets typically project cash flow statements, balance sheets, debt, and statements of sources and use of funds.
3. **Operational budgets:** These usually consist of projected income statements and a series of supporting statements—such as budgeted sales, budgeted production (in detail), budgeted cost of goods sold, budgeted selling expenses, budgeted general and administrative expenses, and, finally, budget for overall sales.

The process often points out conflicts between top management's objectives and the realities of the company's sales capabilities. Through budgeting, management can both identify resources that will be necessary to achieve objectives and learn how those resources must be applied. If present resources cannot meet planned objectives, the process of operational budgeting may bring about an examination of the financial implications of additional asset procurement (capital budgeting).[4]

Companies practice a top-down or bottom-up approach for sales budgeting. The top-down approach is like fitting the sales projections into the number that management needs to operate the business.

Top-down budgeting is a budgeting method in which senior management develops a high-level budget for the company. Once the top-level numbers are created, amounts are allocated to individual functions or departments that must create a detailed budget with their set financial allocation.

Bottom-up budgeting is a type of budgeting that attempts to determine the underlying costs for each individual department or segment of an organization and then total up each department's costs. This type of budgeting works in contrast to top-down budgeting. Which is right and what method is workable for the sales team? There is no right system, and I have worked under both. For the sales team, understanding your funnel potential for the next sales period and forecast reality is imperative for next year's sales. My preference as an ex-company director is a mix of both.

Some companies ask you prior to finalizing next year's sales budgets to conduct a business driver review around September or April and present your individual sales plans. This exercise is often conducted during this budgeting period. The reason why management does this is to test you. They want to see if you know your territory and funnel, to forecast next year's sales growth, including your assessment of the market needs. They will be watching over forecasting too. If you are requested to present your next year's business driver forecasts, please consider showing the following items:

---

[4]Sales Budget: Definition & Examples—by Robert S. 02/14/2018—A great guide for setting up a basic sales budget from the beginning; I highly recommend this training.

- Brief overall summary to begin with, including customer base.
- Introduce your funnel management outcome.
- Break down the number of units to achieve next year's budget.
- Break down the dollars to be forecasted that should meet the unit plan.
- List by region where this growth of sales will come from.
- List promotional growth and its origin of sales.
- List marketing needs to achieve this growth and overall forecast, even down to costs.
- List your overall operating cost less your salary/commission.
- List additional marketing support needed.
- Summarize and close with an optimistic power view.

The key to a business driver is to keep the presentation simple. Avoid any details, but have them ready on the side if needed. Do not overbudget or show unrealistic numbers in sales or territory costs. Ask if the plan is within the management's projections. These numbers should match your CRM opportunities; if not, you are in trouble and not matching the forecast funnel.

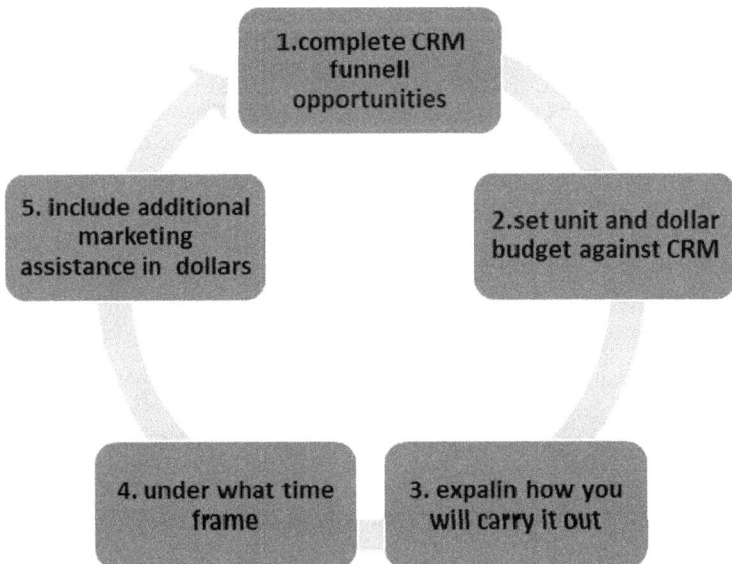

Figure 7.1 Personal territory budget cycle

In Simple Terms, This Is Your Five-Step Guide

I fully support this process. It brings you, the sales individual, back to your area's basics and makes you treat your area as if it is your own business. Remember, if you are a top sales performer, you will find yourself under high expectations. It is important to show right from the start of the presentation that you are following a logical funnel process.

If, for any reason, you forecast a more positive sales plan coupled with your future funnel outlook, management may alter and increase your sales budget accordingly.

What to Do If the Company Sets an Impossible Sales Budget That Causes Conflict?

Companies that do not involve their sales staff in budget forecasting are shortsighted. Returning from Christmas holidays and being given your forthcoming year's sales forecast without any contribution is nothing short of disgraceful management. The act of asking salespeople to achieve a specific sales target without any consultation is arrogant and lacking in any form of team spirit.

How to Prevent Excessive Sales Budgets Set against Your Agreement!

Follow your sales funnel religiously every day and know the details well. Constantly consult your sales manager regarding progress of sales through the year. Ask to submit your forecast sales budget, if not asked.

Submit your sales plan around the final quarter accounting for funnel forecasting, and, finally, request to contribute to all things in your territory. Take ownership.

Setting your future sales plan based on the above logic makes it is hard for the company to refuse or deviate.

Cross-Territory Boundary Encroachment without Notice—How to Prevent Conflict

Nothing gets us more upset than knowing the manager or another sales team member is encroaching on our territory, **without notice**. Hearing this third hand is even more concerning, as when a close customer reports a representative from your company was in the other day.

Companies also conduct customer surveys with your customers through a third-party research company engaged by management. This form of customer feedback is good, but the account manager must know this is going on within their territory.

Cross-territory selling is common in retail as the market is open to peruse your sales. We see that the latest turf war is between major retailers and Internet sales, where it is different in our industry. We are allocated a specific area to represent. Alternatively, in pharmaceutical sales, again it is somewhat convoluted, with doctors prescribing in different practices and different areas, including hospitals. Considering this, where do we draw the line in the sand?

To Prevent Conflict between Team Members over Territorial Boundaries, Consider the Following Suggestions

Know your area and its boundaries and teammates' areas well. Have a clear understanding of territory crossover policy with your sales manager, and if there are identified sales crossed over, have your sales manager identify for budget and commission payments. Ensure you see all orders in your area to document crossover issues, and structure clear agreements with close sales team members regarding boundaries.[5]

Overreaching Your Responsibilities

Being caught up in the day-to-day sales excitement, we sometimes take liberties when offering inducements to secure an order. Call this overconfidence or bravado, but this behavior often puts one outside the operational policies of the company. When I was a national sales manager, I made it very clear to the team: **"no surprises."**
  Some of the rules to follow.

- No entertainment without prior notice to your manager
- Coffee is at the salesperson's discretion

---

[5]Sales Territory Alignment: An Overlooked ... a worthwhile look at this very perplexing problem in sales.

- No additional discount below your approved discount scale level
- No additional customer training without management approval
- No days off without management approval
- No samples given out unless authorized beyond your scale.

Overreaching your salesperson limits is viewed from sales managers, that you are running your own business and bypassing the rules. Don't do this; it is an insult to your manager and can lead to a situation of being reported or sanctioned.

RULE OF THUMB: Stay clean, don't lie, work hard, and be successful.

CHAPTER 8

Ethics in Sales

Is the sales code of ethics effective in our sales world today, and what implications will current and past changes have on selling in the major markets around the world? This chapter deals primarily with ethics in sales and past indiscretions in the pharmaceuticals industry and what has been corrected to prevent the recurrence of such ethical problems.

There has been vigorous debate over whether codes of conduct are an effective mechanism for controlling pharmaceutical and medical sales promotion. This question also applies to all professional selling in general too.

A series of studies by clinical pharmacologists, conducted between 1985 and 1992,[1] led to the conclusion that the quality of information in advertisements had improved.

The emergence of many other activities, such as symposia, and the activities of pharmaceutical representatives, in particular adherence to the Code, have not been well studied. A small study of pharmaceutical representatives' presentations to doctors suggested that the information provided *was not always accurate* or in accordance with the agreed USA Code.

Codes around the world, however, appear to have improved and become more robust since complaints by doctors against pharmaceutical reps were lodged. Telling "porky pies," as we call this, has been to a degree, outlawed for now.

Code of Ethics in Australia/New Zealand Today

Today in Australia, Medicines Australia (MA), a self-regulating body, based out of Canberra, publishes a list of members and breaches of

---

[1] Medicines Australia's Code of Conduct, which was established in 1960, has been revised on a regular basis. Code of Conduct Edition 18.

code of conduct. MA advised me that there were six breaches between 2016/2017 and that four were heard by a committee. For the nonmembers such as generic brand manufacturers, and some drug producers, the GBMA (Generic and Biosimilar Medicines Association), is their overarching governing body, which regulates their ethics and behavior. GBMA is a representative body of generic and biosimilar medicine suppliers in Australia. Its members ensure that all Australians are offered generic and biosimilar medicines of the highest quality in the world together with affordable community health outcomes that benefit all Australians.

It is to be noted that the Surgical Device, Implant, and Capital sectors, represented by the MTAA (Medical Technology Association of Australia), represent the medical technology industry manufacturers and suppliers of nonpharmaceutical products. It is heartening to see such a body of review now available in Australia, following on from the therapeutic Goods Australia (TGA).

Code of Ethics within the United Kingdom

The Ethical Business Practice "code" has been adopted by the ABHI, (Association of British Healthcare Industries). They set the ethical standards for salespeople and for governing ethical promotions by sales professionals and companies. This includes the list of medical products and medical devices. The Code is administered by the ABHI secretariat, comprising the "chairman" and a number of industry representatives. Compliance with the Code and with this Procedure is mandatory for members of ABHI and companies, which, although nonmembers, have agreed to comply with the Code and this procedure and accept the jurisdiction of the panel. "Complaints" this complaint representative body, appears to be a better arrangement as pharmaceutical, medical devices, and hospital products are all covered by the general code of ethics.

It has been said that sponsored private governing bodies that adjudicate complaints from members can be fraught with ethical questions too. To date, the UK code seems to be working efficiently.[2]

---

[2]Code of ethics UK.

Code of Ethics in the United States

With the latest ethics and compliance programs being implemented by the Pharmaceutical Research and Manufacturers of America and the Office of Inspector General, U.S. pharmaceutical sales representatives are once again working in a stricter ethical environment. Industry consultants report pharmaceutical sales reps are laying new emphasis on relationship building. One of the ways in which some sales reps are working to create and strengthen ties with doctors is by positioning themselves as educational resources on narrowly defined therapeutic areas and complicated diseases.

These guidelines will affect long-term behaviors, and some of the trappings will fall away in the short term, but these new codes will ultimately direct behavior because the public outcry over the perception that "pharmaceutical companies are influencing how doctors prescribe drugs has gotten the attention of the Federal Drug Authority (FDA)."[3]

Registration of All Implantable Devices

Currently and during my time in the implant surgical business, the patient registration and implant detail registration security was seen as insufficient and easily hacked by outside influences. I refer to "outside influences" as anybody that can easily access, by stealing or hacking, computer patient records from private implant suppliers or agents on behalf of global manufacturers.

I refer to the following examples:

- Breast implants and other plastic surgery implants for body enhancement
- Injectable implants for incontinence and bulking agents
- Stent implants for cardiac and vascular use
- Stents for esophageal placement
- Orthopedic and general implants

---

[3]Jennifer LeClair, Monster. Health Care Division Bureau of Competition Federal Trade Commission Washington D.C. 20580

- Urology implants for erectile dysfunction and urology implants for incontinence
- Gynecology mesh for incontinence correction and hernia meshes
- Skin grafts and other grafts for cardiac use

There are very many more to list, but my point is this—the registration of all implants used *patient stickers* on each product registration patient form. One was kept by the hospital, one by the manufacturer/distributor and one by the overseas manufacturer, for marketing data collection. Patients' names could be easily accessed at any stage of the product implant postoperative log. What concerns me is whether this slack process has improved or whether private patients' records are still easily accessible.

Patient privacy is protected by statutory law, and any disclosure of this private vital information could be subjected to infringement in all countries that have similar laws of privacy.

This privacy issue did come up as an issue many years ago but was hurriedly dismissed by company importers as it fell into the too hard basket. Logging of patient implants' information is mandatory, but, again, information left on desks is up for grabs.

Security of Patients' Names

When I cite security issues, implant registration patient forms were kept in cars, laptop bags, and on work desks in offices. When the form hit the office, it would lie on a desk for days awaiting data impute and then filed in a folder under date for further reference against a patient warranty claim. So, ultimately, patient implant forms are easily accessible, calling for immediate review of the privacy of patients, unless this area has miraculously cleaned up overnight worldwide. I am told this process has not changed.

In speaking with several management representatives recently, orders placed for an implant to be scheduled for a procedure is accompanied with a patient Number rather than a patient name; this is a much more secure procedure.

Ideally, this process to prevent the patient's identity being disclosed should be followed: patient names stay in the hospital with access allowed only by the implanting doctor. Companies should have no access to patients' names whatsoever! A numbering or codes system would suffice. *End of story.* Patients have the right to privacy.

What Is the Upshot of All of This?

Ethical practices have improved, and companies outside the pharmaceutical business have or should adopt a code if their individual country lacks this legislation.

Even handing out chocolates at product shows is now frowned upon. Giving away company merchandise such as pens, lanyards, and other promotional paraphernalia is not accepted anymore, but the sponsorships of doctors traveling to a clinical meeting overseas is still being practiced worldwide, though under the banner of "education," with travel costs being borne by the company. It seems that companies have restricted their promotional budget on the surface but have diverted these funds in a more and meaningful business manner. In the end, sales reps in the medical industry must look for other innovative ethical ways to sell and promote their products.

Ethics of Sales Representatives Working and Selling in a Clinical Environment

This is a most difficult and profound subject to talk about. Sales reps entering a clinical area such as the operating theater, angiography suite, day procedure, ICU, and any other clinical department should always be clear of sales influence. Having said that, I am as guilty as all others working in the theater.

Over the past 10 years, entry has tightened up, and entry is very restricted but still allowed. Companies get around this by employing qualified clinical specialists to enter these areas as they have the qualifications to do so. Certainly, this is partly true, but most hospitals worldwide permit only visiting medical officers and medical staff in these critical areas.

Reps selling, for example by assisting the doctor technically to implant a stent for example, is riding the bull of disaster today and has no place in our world of selling today.

The Future Possibilities

Be aware, the code of selling ethics in the medical industry may change in the future. As salespeople sell worldwide, draconian rules are likely to be introduced limiting sales calls to only 2 or 3 per year per doctor, this is now happening. Or perhaps sales calls may be allowed only on special occasions such as new product launches, or, worse still, sales calls may be banned altogether and only e-mail material allowed to be circulated. The point here is this: We, as salespeople, continue to twist the product performance truth, continue sponsoring doctors on overseas trips, and so on. This will push regulators to introduce stricter sanctions, thus cutting us out of the picture altogether. It will only take several serious complaints, and it is all over for us as professionals.

One can only imagine a future with no opportunities to deal with, as, for example, private hospital groups seeing only managers from the suppliers and putting us out of the picture to influence customers our way. This leaves us with public hospitals allowing hospital staff and doctors to see reps. This may be challenged soon as hospitals are now gathered into regional groups, with a central buying group supplying the entire area, a measure that would amount to restricting sales reps' activity.

We as professionals, on the ground and inhouse, must realize if we are to survive as an entity, we have to be honest, tow the line and behave in the sales environment. We are at the cross roads of sales person survival and what we do and how we present our business is vital.

CHAPTER 9

Training or the Lack of It

This chapter deals with the concept of sales and product training, in general, backed up with the overall research carried out in Australia and overseas. The decline of comprehensive training and a move toward e-training methods is disturbing. I put this down to taking the easy way out, namely, relying on students of this craft, learning from a screen. I have no objection to e-training being mixed in with the training curriculum; however, training coaches using this format as the primary learning method are short-sighted in their own craft of coaching. They themselves are in need of re-training.

Importance of Combining Product and Sales Training

Both product training and sales skill training are important to increase the knowledge and expertise of individual sales team members. Which of the two, however, is more important? Which has the larger impact? Before I answer that question, let me define the differences between the two training methods to make sure that we are all on the same page. These can both be conducted simultaneously, and how do we measure the overall productivity?

Product Training on Its Own

Product training focuses on the nuts and bolts and technical product information and features—educating your sales force on the functionality of what the company sells, specifically, what the product (or service or solution) is, what problems it's intended to solve, how it actually works, and what it costs in its various configurations. Product training should also include competitive products as a measure of what you are up against in the market. In addition, product training provides a sense of company understanding and what philosophy the organization stands for. Finally product training ensures the sales person and there intermate knowledge of what they sell.

Sales Training on Its Own

Sales training, on the other hand, is less about the product than about how to help the prospect or customer relate the product's capabilities to their needs. Most products and services these days need to be configured or applied, tailored, integrated in some fashion in order to maximize the ROI, (return on investment,) that the client sees in their purchase. In other words, it's about creating value for your customer.

As a result, sales skill training teaches how to converse with the prospect about their needs and how to collaborate on solutions. The goal is to give sales people the confidence to go out and discuss "how" their products can be used to deliver results. The ideal environment for sales skill training is small groups that promote interactivity, application of what has been learned, and group discussion along with active role-play.

As we have discussed in previous chapters, in-house sales training is useless without field sales coaching on a regular basis; anybody that argues otherwise is either not qualified to coach or is in a 60's mindset.

So, can you bring together both, product training and sales training? Yes, as long as field coaching is conducted soon after.

Longer-Term Value of Training

Research has found that about 85 percent of sales training has no lasting impact after 120 days. This is a serious concern and puts into question why we conduct training in the first place. Yet companies are spending billions of dollars worldwide on sales training each year. A consideration of the sales training dollars being spent is overwhelming. CSO Insights conducted a study in which they segmented the data on the basis of how sales organizations rated their sales training programs. CSO Insights found that only over 9 percent of the respondents rated their sales training programs as having "exceeded expectations," while 33 percent rated them as having just "met expectations." The largest category was "needed improvement," at 53 percent.

Sadly enough, this percentage of sales people failing to get what they needed from their sales training is a direct indictment of sales training companies and company leaders delivering the wrong training courses.[1]

The Importance of General Product Knowledge

Product knowledge is the most important tool for leading and closing business. It instills faith, trust, and respect in the customer, creating a positive customer experience. I call this the *me* in selling. In addition, product knowledge correctly aligned with customer needs creates a closer partnership.

Answering Customers' Questions with a Degree of Confidence

Answering difficult questions without adequate product knowledge shows you up as someone deficient in product knowledge. Yes, you can say I will get back to you soon with the answer, but if this becomes routine, then you need to readdress product knowledge as soon as possible.

Today's product training is in many cases fragmented, utilizes on-line training courses, and deliberately removes the one-on-one training needed to field specific questions that come up during the training sessions. Online training can be good, and I have often incorporated this type of training. However, without a mentor or trainer in the flesh, you are not sure if the direction you are going in is the correct one. Training doubts and unanswered questions slow down training, and information is not connected.

Product knowledge tests are vital but have lately been turned into "select one of the following four answers." How much luck is involved in this type of test? I would prefer that test answers be put into sentences rather than just picking the selected answer. Having the actual product in

---

[1] By Norman Behar, interpreted from this paper—CSO Insights. A great paper which pulls apart training and exposes the down and upside of coaching.

our hands and seeing and playing with it is vital to the brain association and formulation of a sales presentation mode.

Competency Based Training

As a competency-based trainer, to me there is no other way to train. In the end as a student you need to explain what the answer is and not take a stab at a selection of 4 answers. Having the key knowledge ensures the company has at least done their job of product knowledge.

See, Touch, Fiddle, Play with Is Real Learning

Studying from a manual is, to a degree, limited until the product materializes and you are able to see the product in action. The combination of feel, touch, volume size, color, and mechanical workings puts together a picture each student needs. Progressing from this point onward is far easier to dig deeper into this product knowledge process.

Is There a Need for Qualified Sales and Product Coaches?

I urge all coaches and sales managers who do not hold a Cert 4 in T&A (training and assessment) to incorporate continual verification testing (CVT). Having a design, training, and assessment qualification sets the coach up for competency-based training and can issue a certificate of learning and competency, legally. Any person in a coaching or training position must have this qualification now. If you are being trained by a coach that does not have a Cert 4 in T&A, then bring it up for discussion.

What If You Feel Your Training Is Insufficient?

If you feel your training is insufficient to progress to the field for full-on sales engagement, tell your mentor or coach that you do not feel adequately ready for field sales. List the specific areas to review. Provide this list to your coach and see what response it brings. You will get one of the following responses:

1. That's great, but your training has been completed, and you will need to pick up knowledge some other way. (they are saying time has run out sorry).
2. We will put you on the next training course in 3 months for review; you start next week in the field. (saying see how you go and bring back questions in 3 months).
3. We understand; next week, we will schedule several more days to bring you up to date. Thank you for bringing this to my attention.

One does not need to spell out the right answer. If you do not receive the right answer, keep asking. If, however, your company refuses to listen, then this sends you a clear message they are not interested in the quality of their representatives.[2]

Should I Study at Night during Training?

I see no reason why a little post-days training review wouldn't be useful. It needn't be hours of review but just a recap of the material and making a few notes to help ask for clarification the next day. Training is not just about sitting there and taking in lots of information; allowing time out to review on your own time and making additional notes is smart. If however, you are not getting the product message, review back and start again.

Taking Training from the School Room to the Field

Are corporate sales training courses failing to translate into real wins for sales?

Many salespeople do like attending sales training courses; however, when it comes to their boss or coach working in the field, they "cringe."

When you scan the web, you find a wealth of sales training courses available, with a variety of styles and "proven selling methods." Very few, if any, disclose the failure rate of their selling method, but commonly, a

---

[2]The current state of sales training US. Lack of Corporate Training as #1 Driver of the "Skills Gap" Sept 2015/This paper makes a clear case for the need for effective sales training.

sales coach or qualified sales manager working with sales team members in the field has significant results, not only in sales but also in selling skills and happiness. However, our local research study indicates that a high proportion of companies fail to provide ongoing field sales training. Most respondents said that their direct manager worked with them only once every 6 months, if that. This is alarming! If your sales manager or coach is being seen only once every 6 months, ask why?

Out into the Field for the First Time

Stay calm and trust yourself to perform.

Many managers in this circumstance tend to let you go to see what you have absorbed and fumble around. Far too many companies (especially agents or distributorships) lead this way and take shortcuts on this very important training need; in fact, I think in some companies, induction seems to play a more important role than product training; my research showed this clearly. Induction played a greater role than comprehensive product training.

What your company is doing is saving money by expecting you to fumble around, make all the mistakes, and come back with a list of product questions. This process is widespread and needs to be stopped. The research found that only a few global organizations carried out training differently.

One example of this stringent training system was the one followed by a surgical company selling tissue staplers. Training in this company was often carried out overseas. The reason was that they were not employing sales staff primarily from the medical profession, in general, so clinical and surgical training was imperative to sell in this space. This did set the benchmark for product training; the only restrictive element was the cost.[3]

What Does the Customer Expect from Your Product Knowledge?

In my own experience, customers, have indicated to me, they expected the following from their salesperson:

---

[3]Preparing New Sales Reps for Success: The Importance of On-the-Job Field Training and Coaching/May 1, 2017Taryn Oesch, CPTM0

- Honesty regarding product performance.
- Truthful representation of the product and its capabilities and availability of the product.
- Respect for the customer's time and avoidance of the tendency to knock the competitor
- Meeting the customer by appointment instead of making cold calls, and avoiding being pushy; also, following up quickly with the customer's request.

The key fundamental here is product knowledge and sales attitude. If you have product knowledge and can answer key product questions without having to refer to an iPad, you have automatically improved your customer respect level. A good hint is not to over answer or oversupply information. Answer the customer's questions and be alert to customer needs.

An example of over answering customer questions is the salesperson spewing out product performance or features and benefits without keeping a few in reserve for a later date.

A More Detailed Examination of Training

Sixty-nine per cent of Australian survey respondents said their company did not provide appropriate product or sales training. Of those respondents, the majority said they did not receive appropriate product training fitting the customer's need. Of the remainder, 31 percent said their product training could have been much better. A very small percentage said their product training was sufficient.[4]

Not one research respondent said their training was outstanding or comprehensive.

As a sales coach, I firmly believe the two are intertwined at inception. I do not believe you can separate the two unless it is, for example, sales process update training, drawing out a specific sales skill to learn. This is greatly dependent on when and where. Both product and sales training cohere well together when the new salesperson is undergoing initial training. Product update and sales training can thereafter be separated and carried out on the basis of a specific need. This process is based on

---

[4]Australian research.

the frequency of salesperson turnover, skill level of selling, and the rate of product information uptake. New product introductions come and go, so bringing together both sales and product training is a natural process. Separating the both is a fruitless exercise.

Where Else Are We Failing with Training?

Many sales training programs neglect to provide a process and methodology that salespeople can follow to systematically move prospects through the pipeline. Without a process or methodology, training gets forgotten, and salespeople end up reinventing the wheel over and over again. For instance, if your sales manager is your coach, expect that the manager will give you limited time in the field; this is a fact seen every day in sales. I recommend that you be persistent if you are not getting attention. Keep asking for further training, and be specific in regard to the area you need to review.

Why Is Sales Training Not Universal and Consistent?

Working for 4 global companies in my career, not one sales training course was consistent with any other. The versions did differ greatly and as time went on, RTO's came up with many different sales training themes so they were seen as new and exciting. Without having to mention the key sales training themes, they are all talking about the seven steps of the sale in their own format. To have sales training globally uniform would be impossible as too many RTOs what the business of training and will sell their own brand.

Failure to Deliver Training That Engages

Salespeople are known to leave training programs, saying things like:

"Boring, needed to engage all of us"
"Not applicable, what are they doing, it is not what I needed"
"The instructor wasn't so hot, did not inspire me, seemed to be on another planet"

"What a waste of time, should have been at work selling"

Very few salespeople say that their training was exceptional and gave them a shot in the arm to go out there and put the new information into action. However, I have heard on a rare occasion, students saying "that was great".

The Place of Role-Play in Training Now—Competency Training—Positive or Negative?

Adults learn by practicing, and you need a training program that engages and gets salespeople to put the new skills to use. It must also be relevant to their skill needs. This is where role-play is important. Gone are the days of sitting for hours and being lectured to for meager results.

My early memories of being picked out to do role-play was daunting, and if you performed badly, management would single you out for a serving. This leaves you crumpled but does not help you realize you have to do better. As a coach, I have used role-play on a regular basis, putting myself up first to show how it is done. Leading by example is necessary to conduct training effectively. Sales coaches should demonstrate how it is done first before asking the group to follow themselves.

Role-play is generally detested by salespeople as it leaves them with a degree of anxiety waiting to be called up next. What I suggest is to put your hand up first, offering to do a role-play with the boss or another colleague. My thought is to get it over first so you can sit back and relax for the rest of the session.[5] Embrace role play as it puts you right into the actual sales situation.

Follow-Up Field Training Is Essential to Cement the Overall Message

Without reinforcement, salespeople forget learned skills and knowledge and how inspired and motivated they were, with the result that the learning effectiveness decreases.

---

[5]Posted by Carole Mahoney/The science of role play to improve sales.

It is a sales manager's responsibility to conduct follow-up training. A sales manager should work with each team member *3 days per month and no less*, depending on the team size. If you have a sales manager that never rides with you in the field, he or she is doing both of you an injustice. Having the company pay very high fees for outside training courses is criminal if the sales manager or coach is not conducting a structured post-training-field coach session. The more they work with you, the better sales improve.

Failures of Evaluation, Accountability, and Continuous Improvement

Few companies actually evaluate the effectiveness of their sales or product training. Sales training can fail simply because companies have no idea if it has succeeded or not. Furthermore, without evaluation, it's nearly impossible to hold salespeople accountable for changing and improving behavior or for taking actions and achieving results.

The end result of this problem is low sales results. When this happens, fingers are pointed at the sales managers and sales staff, not at the lack of appropriate sales training. The blame for low sales always falls on the sales person or poorest performer and not up the ladder, where approval of poor training is signed off—from top downward.

A good coach should plot incremental salesperson improvement and plan field training days to cover off on specific sections required for performance. Sales managers, on the other hand, do not and have a lot of time to operate such complicated training methods. As a sales person, you need to explore your improvement and log your training future needs.

Your Skills and Performance and How They Are Plotted

Your sales performance is generally plotted by your sales manager in a confidential file. Progress, sales results, new customer opportunities, team cooperation, closing sales, and general knowledge of product and sales process are just a few items you are judged on; including your personal profile is also kept in human resources. Reviews of this information are updated and produced for a formal performance review either once or twice a year.

Apart from your sales results, you should, during your one-on-one meeting with your manager, be honest and candid.

Working in the Field Training—The Best Place for Fun

Field coaching is the most important training of all. As pointed out in this chapter, we tend not to do training well; however, if we do it reasonably, then why waste all the time and money by not measuring the results.

These results of field training, are measured in three ways:

1. Overall sales results
2. Sales performance assessment matrix sheet
3. Salesperson satisfaction

When you feel you are adequately skilled and trained for your sales job and have a good and ever-improving product knowledge base under your belt, the job function seems much more enjoyable and satisfying. For those that have not experienced this field coaching style, it goes like this: Your manager will arrange a day or several days together in the field meeting customers. A good manager will ask you to prepare a mix of new and existing customers to sell to. Make the appropriate arrangements, and prepare your car, selling tools, updated customer information, and day's sales objectives. Be very careful to review each sales call later with your manager. The review critique process is discussed later in the book for study reference. Also make sure you know where your customer resides, being late is a no in coaching.

A Notable Example of Poor Preparation Visit

When coaching interstate in my last coaching position, I arranged the above and was picked up at my hotel at 8 a.m. The salesperson did not provide me with the day's agenda, but only confirmed the pickup time. The day progressed without an agenda .The salesperson said that this next sales call was their largest customer and that he knew the account "like the back of his hand." We were to visit the nurse unit manager in intensive care. When we arrived, he proceeded to look at the ground floor address board for the ICU floor, and we took the elevator to the third floor, as instructed. He walked out of the lift and hesitated, not knowing whether to turn left or right.

What Do We Learn about This Common Situation?

The representative did not know his key account at all, down to the floor the ICU account was on and the direction to take on the third floor. Even the most astute representative would have done a pre-reconnaissance a week before to make sure about the floor and position of their customer, avoiding embarrassment on the day. Note that the day's activities were confirmed a month in advance.

What we learn from this is that you must cover off on preparation right down to the basics; you need to be clear about where to drive and how to locate your customer and identify who is your target. Never go ahead without sending your coach or manager a day's agenda a week ahead.

Check off the following tips if your boss or coach is spending a day in the field with you soon.

- Agree on date and time for fieldwork with your boss or trainer.
- Have agreed appointments set up and copy your boss or coach.
- Do a small sales plan for each sales customer visit and an objective outcome.
- Be on time for customer visits, plan sales call visit distances carefully.
- Make sure your iPad or device is well charged.
- Introduce your boss to the customer, and then engage the customer in conversation.
- Keep in mind the key sales training points you need to show.
- Remember that you, not the coach, are in charge of the sales call.
- Post sales call, you should perform a critique so you are able to show where you did well and where you could improve, then engage your coach.

- Endeavor to show improvement for the next sales call.
- Always be aware of your sales plan and monthly budget with your manager, and be able to identify where you can see sales to plug the gap.
- Do not drive to the next sales call until you have completed your own critique.
- At the end of the day, discuss with your manager or coach key items to work on.
- Always accept training and coaching advice.

If you can follow the foregoing ideas, you will do very well.

How Do We Stack Up as Sales Trainers versus Our Overseas Counterparts?

Sales training as it is today appears not to be working. The e-learning industry reports that 47 percent of training hours were delivered by instructor-led classroom setting, suggesting that face-to-face training seems to be declining. It is much easier to ask students to watch a video or take an e-training course that frees up management's time. Believe it or not, this number increased 3 percent as compared with that in the previous year, and one would suggest that in 2020, it would be greater. The yearly spend on sales training is increasing year after year. American companies are spending about twenty billion dollars a year on sales training, but I wonder how much is spent on follow-up field training. A lot of companies are making huge profits from engagement in such training. This is not accounting for in-house company-based sales training; some companies use both.

No major sales enablement initiatives taken	12.6%
Meet few of our expectations	11.25
Meet some of our expectations	44.8%
Meet or exceeded the majority of expectations	26.1%
Nil	5.25%

Figure 9.1 Sales training engagement

Miller Heiman Group makes a case for sales training and have published results saying that training from outside companies "meet some of our expectations." Only 26 percent of the survey exceeded the majority of expectations, and many reported few or low initiatives taken home.

From the salesperson's point of view, your company will choose the registered training organization (RTO) to come in and run sales training. With regard to product training, your company will, generally, perform such training. The sheer fact that your company is employing outside sales training says several things. For example, the company is not equipped to perform sales training from within, and it relies on outside RTOs to keep up to date with current market sales trends.

How Do We Improve Training?

Improvement starts with management and budgeting. Sales and product training are core functions, apart from securing sales. Training and sales go hand in hand, but some companies see this differently, even to the point of diminishing the need to train, usually for budgetary reasons (which is understandable) or not having a trainer in-house. However, leaving sales staff to their own devices in the field allows bad habits to continue and become entrenched with the end result of the wrong company message being passed on.

Sales results continue to diminish, and field happiness diminishes to the point where either a few leave or many leave en masse. One company I was close to during the 2015 to 2017 period lost over thirty-five sales staff nationally for a myriad of reasons, including gross unhappiness, poor sales, overbearing senior management, overpricing and not being competitive, and a feeling of superiority to others. Customers picked up on this and started to abandon the product.

Tick Off Some of These Suggestions When Applying for a New Position

When seeking to join a new company for the first time, make a list of important questions regarding training. Some of the following questions may get you offside, but you have a right to seek the information. These questions can be asked closer to the selection time, perhaps when the company has you present for a third interview.

- How long is the training period? This depends on how technical the products are.
- Do I need to go interstate or overseas for training?
- Is training partly in-house and partly in the field?
- How long do I need to be in field training before running solo with customers?
- What level of knowledge do I need as a minimum to go solo with customers?
- What level of selling skills do I need to go solo?
- Is the training competency based or theory based or both; are there tests involved?
- Who will be the trainer, and are they adequately qualified?

The last point is contentious but necessary. Perhaps you can find this out in another way.[6]

In conclusion, training provides you with all the basic requirements that will give you some confidence in the product you are about to sell for many years to come. You have to know a lot about your product to be sales savvy and successful. Here, we are talking about pure product knowledge and product performance along with its limitations.

Once you know the basics, then sales training incorporating your competitors and their features and benefits with a selling program aligned to your products gives you an early start to engage the customer.

Without this early quality start, engagement with your customer base will oblige you to play catch-up forever. Your customers will know that you are guessing all the time and turn their back on you. However, if your product knowledge and selling skills are honed well, you will sell very well.

---

[6]By Ashok Sharma/May 10, 2017/Corporate learning 5 Key Strategies to Improve Sales Training and Development Within Your organization/Simply, this paper describes five ways to improve sales training. Keeping it simple, following this example, is fundamentally sound.

CHAPTER 10

What Is Your *Me Brand* and Selling Style?

This chapter helps you identify your selling style and discover your *Me* Brand. It also helps you identify the positive selling habits and the bad habits you need to work on. Finally, it teaches you the best psychological frame of mind you need to be in to sell successfully.

Six Selling Styles—Which Is Yours?

As easy as it looks, there is more to selling than you think. It is very important to know the -type of salesperson you are. Unfortunately, this will not become apparent for several years into your sales career. If you sell outside your primary selling style regularly, you are in danger of becoming unsuccessful. Once you know your style, you're likely to seek out sales positions that take advantage of your strengths and minimize your weaknesses. Different personalities will have different selling styles. In what follows, I have outlined what I believe are the five common selling styles.

1. **Aggressive selling:** This is one of those styles where the sales rep stays highly focused and the only intention is to sell and walk out with the order. The salesperson with such a sales method indulges in a hard-driving selling style; he or she does not believe in the so-called "sales cycle process" but tries to get the job done in one shot. A clear example of this style is car sales.
2. **Relationship builder:** The relationship-building selling style is widely regarded as the most successful of all selling styles globally. However, this is in contrast to some overseas research. The sales

person here indulges in a type of method where they adjust well to any kind of selling situation (chameleon personality). It does not matter to them whether the prospect is in line to become a buyer or not.

3. **Need-oriented selling and challenger style:** This is the kind of selling style where you need to think quickly and adapt. The salesperson needs to be highly tactful and at the same time be able to ask questions aimed at finding out what the customer needs. In simple terms, this selling style is about learning more about the client's existing needs rather than about creating new ones.

4. **Product-oriented selling:** With product-oriented selling style, the sales rep is more inclined toward explaining fully the features and benefits of the product to the prospect. This style includes a lot of product demo until the prospect is fully convinced of the benefits. But there is a danger of overloading the prospect with information.

5. **Competition-oriented and persistent selling:** The competition-oriented salesperson is very persistent in trying to persuade a potential customer. Overcoming objections by never taking a no for an answer or not knowing when to back off (as with No 1), they will do everything possible to close a deal, resulting in direct and interpersonal influence.

6. **Be a chameleon seller:** The best salespeople vary their selling style according to the customer and the situation. Although questioning and listening, asking for the order, and product knowledge are all important, what is more important is knowing when to use each of these skills and techniques. That is what I mean by selling style flexibility. This style takes a little of each of six styles and uses it according to the circumstances.

In summary, there's no single best sales approach. Your personality and background ethnicity will determine the type of sales technique that is most effective for you. Even if you have a methodology that works well, it's a good idea to try a different approach now and then. Trying new methods keeps you out of a rut, and you may be surprised how well a new sales approach works for you. In fact, many salespeople do best by using a combination of approaches.

How to Assess Your Current Selling Style

If you are still confused about your selling style, then try this simple test:

- Are you a confident or outgoing personality, type A or type B?
- Are you driven or laidback?
- Do you believe in your product or service or not that interested?
- What is your style out of the six listed above, or are some morphed together?
- Are you driven to see as many new prospects or not?
- Are you afraid of prospecting; does this scare you too much?
- Do you constantly call on your favorite customers and avoid difficult clients?
- Do your see your customers as friends or opportunities for sales?
- When doing cold calls or planned sales calls, do you get excited?
- Can you identify each style in your sales team?
- Are you willing to try different styles, and what are they?
- Can you flip between several sales styles?

If you are unable to answer many of the foregoing questions about your sales style, you need assistance. In this case, ask your mentor or sales manager you work with in the field to tell you how close you are to the six styles and to identify how they can assist you in style improvement. However, if you are confused and unable to select a specific style, ask another seller that knows you.

My "*Me Brand*"

Over your career, you will get to be known by many customers, and you, as a seller, will develop a *Me Brand*, which is independent of your company and products. This *Me Brand* follows you from job to job, given that you stay in the one-industry domain.

Are Selling Styles Different in Varying Industries?

Yes; however, I fully believe the industry you sell in tends to shape a particular style. An example of a particular style is selling neonatal products to neonatal nursing staff. It requires a quiet, understanding, and specific sales style. Selling power tools to shops, on the other hand, may require a very different style.

Subsections of these six personality styles are shown further:

1. **The instant buddy:** People feel better about buying from someone they like. Salespeople who use the buddy approach are warm and friendly, ask questions, and show interest in their prospects. They try to connect on an emotional level with each prospective customer, in a manner that somewhat resembles the relationship style.

2. **The guru and ultimate expert:** Salespeople who prefer a more logical and less emotional approach set themselves the task of becoming experts in anything and everything related to their specific industry. They position themselves as problem-solvers, able to answer any question and tackle any issue that the prospect lays before them.

3. **The consultant:** This approach combines the "guru" and "buddy" approaches. The salesperson who elects to use the consultant approach presents themselves as an expert who has the customer's best interests in mind. They know all about the company's products, and by asking a prospect a few questions, they can match them with the best product for their needs.

4. **The networker:** Networking can be a big help for any salesperson. The dedicated networker takes it to the next level, setting up and maintaining a web of friends, coworkers, salespeople from other companies, customers, and former customers, and anyone else he/she meets. A strong enough network will create an ongoing flow of warm leads that can provide most or even all of the salesperson's needs. It also supports your *Me Brand* awareness. The networker approach is practiced by realtor professionals as a primary business driver. An example of this is Real-estate sales.

5. **The hard-dogged seller:** Best described as "scare the prospect into buying," the hard sell approach is what gives salespeople a bad reputation. Hard selling involves getting someone to buy a product even though he or she doesn't want or need it. Relying on methods ranging from bullying ("Buy this now, or you'll feel stupid tomorrow") to manipulation ("If you don't buy from me, I'll lose my job") to

outright deception, this substyle appears to be a sad story if one has to operate as such.

6. **Pushing the bruise:** Sadly, there are still salespeople who use this type of sales strategy, even though it results in a customer who never buys again and, sooner or later, a bad reputation for the company as a whole. A selling example that is taught by several registered training organizations (RTOs) and is part of the selling "probing stage" and uses the term *pushing the bruise* so the customer visualizes what the future would be if they don't buy. In all seriousness, customers know what will be if they don't buy.

After finding out the customer's needs, the needs payoff question is posed:

> So, if you are not able to purchase this new plastic molding machine by next month, what implications will show up; will you have to cut back on new projects?

In other words, drawing out concern, fear, and other emotions to move the customer faster to purchase. I have used this technique but only in selective situations. Used in the wrong situation, the customer becomes suspicious of the salesperson's motive. We call this type of selling "needs payoff sales," and it is used by a global education company as a cornerstone probing technique. I have no objection to using this technique, but if it goes wrong, you are set back tremendously.[1]

Seven Other Ways to Look at Selling Styles

There is more to selling than you think. These interesting styles are more product- and customer-related styles.

1. **Competition-oriented selling:** The competition-oriented salesperson tends to be pushy and is continually referring and comparing his or product with an immediate competitor's, without being prompted. It shows the salesperson is acutely aware of the competition and not

---

[1]Five types of Selling Styles – Which One is Yours? /A good paper to study about the various selling styles we see worldwide.

confident about selling his or her own product confidently. Do not follow this style at all; it is prompted when a competitor has the upper hand in the market and the seller is worried about their competition getting ahead.

2. **Image-oriented selling:** These kinds of professionals ooze credibility and stand out from the crowd. The salesperson sells himself or herself first and the product last. It is a twisted style that does not demonstrate product knowledge and what the needs of the customer are. Personal image becomes paramount to the sale; again, I do not recommend this style.

3. **Need-oriented selling:** This salesperson is highly tactful and quick to ask relevant questions to discover and understand the customer's needs. It makes a good start provided it begins with background planning to reduce the incessant pressure of questioning on the customer. Probing is part of the seven steps of the sale, but keep it short as the customer will become aggravated if you practice this technique too much. Customers will only answer so many probing questions then they will turn off.

4. **Product-oriented selling:** The sales person knows all the features and benefits of a product or service. Again, this style is OK, but some salespeople overload the customer with their incredible knowledge of everything. Customer overload can lead to rejection of you and your company. Make it reflective of the customer needs only. The sales person wants to impress their customer with the ever-ending knowledge, again boring.

5. **Rapport-oriented selling:** Building and developing long-term relationships is the key characteristic of this type of sales person. We call this third-party selling as it involves saying, "My last customer also uses product X and is happy." If you use rapport selling, make sure you have permission and that the customer you are referring to is a happy customer; try to see the situation from the customer's perspective.

6. **Service-oriented selling:** Explains the terms of the contract and leaves this as the feature and benefit all up. This technique disregards customer needs and wants. It should be part of the sales offering, not the whole selling pitch.

7. **Pain-in-the-Butt seller:** This type of seller is more common than you think and adopts many of the preceding traits, mixing them

together to become the most annoying person you have met. Customer's reaction to such persons is not to see them again.

Companies usually use selling style profile analysis tools for career development on an individual basis, for development of sales teams, or for an understanding of sales manager preferences in relation to their role in the company. Whatever your style, remember some of your natural selling styles you're born with; build on those, but don't change your natural personality as this is your first and most important style.

If I Don't Have a Selling Style, How Come I Am Selling Well?

First, if you are selling well, you should be able to assess your personal sales style. Most good salespeople say that if they are selling well, they don't need to change anything—just steady as she goes.

Suggestion

Do some homework and come up with a style you are comfortable with. Every sales person has a style or combination of styles. *It is important to identify which style is yours.* Once you identify a style or a combination of several, try to analyze these, and ask your coach or mentor to discuss them with you one-on-one. If you are doing well in sales, this is fantastic; look at change only for the better and take it bit by bit. There is always room for personal improvement, so embrace this concept.

Why Do I Need a Specific Sales Style?

First, the sales style you have is influenced by your upbringing, interpersonal skills, schooling and education, and your ability to understand how we behave in all situations. Other key influences are the amount of study you put into how customers behave and why. This basic understanding is imperative to formulate your style. Some salespeople just "let it happen." Some others have to work hard on this skill. Either way, you must understand why you do things the way you do them.

It is very embarrassing to do a sales role play and look at yourself selling later on. You are firstly amazed of your voice tone, the way you move, your look and the style you adopt.

A customer can easily tell an unskilled sales person by his or her lack of ability to answer key product questions or understand their needs, habit of not responding to tasks replies, and tendency to avoid the customer when things get too intense.

My Own Style

I have a consultative style. However, I have developed several other skills. Without thinking about this too much, I am always keen to know customer needs first. Once I have the customer's attention, I demonstrate my degree of knowledge to assist them. In sum, I go in as a consultant and, to a degree, as a networker, finishing up with the ability to come back again and be welcomed. Determination and perseverance, I am told, is my best quality.

Importance of Determination in Sales

I cannot emphasize this enough: Determination is probably the most important quality for all salespeople to acquire. I am specifically talking about your inner determination. When you are new and learning the craft, one major quality that will carry you through is the sheer determination to succeed. If, however, you are not this determined person, realizing this shortcoming will help you understand why perhaps you are not getting all the sales you could.

What Psychological Frame of Mind Should I Have for Professional Sales?

It is no secret that sales managers want to see their sales team "on song," "at it hard," "willing to go the extra mile," "bring home the bacon," and "get the business" and many other phrases they like to throw at you.[2]

---

[2]Selling Styles for Successful Salespeople - *Posted on 06/20/2008 in Selling Skills/Again, this posting discusses why we need a sales selling style and its importance for customers.*

Psychologists have many answers for not being "on song" and offer many strategies and treatments for low-performing behavior, even to the point of prescribing pills. If you find your job is uninteresting, lacks challenge, or does not fulfill any of your professional sales needs and interests, perhaps you are in the wrong position. However, if you are the opposite and love your job but have lost the enthusiasm, it is time to refresh and get back into sales mode.

To assess your frame of mind, answer the following questions.

Frame-of-Mind Personal Test

1. Do you look forward to going to work to sell?	yes	no
2. Do you enjoy meeting your customer base?	yes	no
3. Do you enjoy prospecting new customers?	yes	no
4. Do you enjoy good sales results?	yes	no
5. Do you have a good relationship with your sales manager?	yes	no
6. Does your company provide you with product and sales training?	yes	no
7. Are you tired every day and every morning?	yes	no
8. Are you taking sick leave regularly?	yes	no
9. Do you enjoy the company of your colleagues?	yes	no
10. Do you enjoy sales meetings?	yes	no
11. Do you believe in your product or products?	yes	no
12. Do you feel you are in burnout mode?	yes	no

If you answer no to questions 1, 2, 3, 5, 9, 10, 11, you need to review your job position. If you answer yes to questions 7 and 12, then you need to seek help.[3]

Digging Deeper

If you said yes to question 12 (you feel you are burnt out), note that burnout syndrome is a treatable condition and should be managed by

---

[3]How to Adopt a Sales Mindset - Thirteen simple rules to become your own sales superstar. This paper puts forward a specific mindset we need for professional selling—a good paper to review.

a professional such as a medical doctor or psychologist. If you answered no to question one (you don't look forward to going to work to sell), not responding to work and sales is a position and job dislodgement. Not looking forward to working is a pointer to many psychological issues, including depression and an aversion to the job in general.

If you answered yes to question eight (taking additional sick leave), it means you have either a psychological or a medical issue or you are using the sick leave because of job disenchantment.

We could examine all these issues and more for many paragraphs, but if you are generally unhappy at work/sales, perhaps looking at another profession instead would be advisable. Even in some circumstances, changing sales companies can do the trick. If you are treading water or spinning the wheels but not gaining traction, it is time to consider whether you want to continue with unhappiness or move on. A word of warning: If you are unhappy, talk to an independent mentor first.

So, in the end, what frame of mind do you need to sell successfully? Have a look at the following list.

- You need to enjoy selling to strangers and new prospects as well as to look forward to the challenge of meeting targets and budgets; having fun with your customers; building up a loyal customer base; and using every selling situation to gain valuable sales experience.
- You need to enjoy working in a tight sales team and being trained for product and sales skills while showing your inner enthusiasm at work; take pride in being friendly and helpful to your customer base, but constantly look for better opportunities to improve your sales skills.
- You need to balance your health and fitness and keep a clear mind and perspective, while avoiding being caught up in intracompany politics.
- You should not get caught up and depressed with sales losses and not be affected by losing a big sale, but should be able to bounce back the next new day.
- You should see the good in your job and avoid the negatives while enjoying building your *Me Brand*.

If you are saying yes to many of the above points, you are on the right track and in a good frame of mind.

What Is Professional Selling, and Why Do We Distinguish This Term?

What Is the Meaning of Professionalism?

A professional seller, in comparison with an amateur salesperson, is one who is being paid for his or her services and is engaged in representing a company that sells reputable products or services.

Alternatively, are we saying that a real estate salesperson is not a professional seller? In general, estate agents are paid on a full commission basis and in some cases are provided with a minimal weekly allowance, which is deducted out of a commissionable sale.

One could say yes, they are professional salespeople, but, on the other hand, they are paid only when they make a sale.

When asked in a friendly group setting, "What do you do for a living?" do you cringe or answer with pride, "I am in sales" and then watch for the reaction?

Why Are We Watching for the Reaction?

Probably because we are not sure how other people or professionals view us in sales? Do they take us to be car salespersons, or are we possibly embarrassed we are not as good as they are? I am not sure about you, but I have felt this at some time of my life, despite having been at the highest possible level of medical and surgical sales.

I believe the term "professional selling" has very little value because its use is highly subjective and context driven. To distinguish the sales value of a person selling tools from that of one selling health equipment can be seen as elitism, but, fundamentally, there is a product and knowledge-level difference. So are we saying you must be more intelligent and have better skills to sell higher-end products?

In my case, I might associate "professional" with "responsible for selling the product." In another conversation and context, I might associate "professional" with "qualified" or "knowledgeable." In yet another, I might comment on a person's lack of professionalism because he/she failed to meet the company standards for salesmanship or behavior, as, for example, not listening to what the buyer was saying.

The person buying trade tools requires the right advice just as much as a person buying fertilizer for farming. The wrong advice in this scenario could be costly. Are we distinguishing between the level of understanding a customer needs and the need for sales knowledge?

I have always thought the term "sales professional" was often used for compensatory reasons. I don't call myself a sales professional, but I am a professional who sells. Yes, I am a sales professional and proud of it.

What Are Bad Selling Habits?

Falling into bad habits generally occurs early in your sales career. During the first 2 to 3 years without field coaching, bad habits form unconsciously, and unless picked up by a good coach, some bad habits are very difficult to turn around and require a personal willingness to alter behavior.

What Are Some Selling Bad Habits to Look Out for?

To break bad habits in sales, begin by defining the behavior you want to change and, with the help of a coach, identifying what triggers that behavior. Then create a concrete plan to change the behavior, and ask someone to hold you accountable.

Work habits are regular patterns of behavior you unconsciously exhibit in your job or place of employment. These habits become part of your routine behavior and are generally an unconscious part your day-to-day sales processes; you may not even be aware of them. This can be a concern as the habit is so ingrained that your awareness becomes completely closed.

So ingrained are the bad habits that you perform the sales process and do not even notice that the customer is taking note! A customer may react to a bad habit by showing surprise or shutting down with their attention or even listening to you but thinking, "This person will never get through my door again."

Even the simplest bad habit such as blinking, sitting incorrectly, overdoing the makeup, dressing inappropriately, and sniffing can turn a customer away in a minute.

My challenge to you? Fight like hell against those sneaky bad habits, and keep them from eroding your hard work. The longer you ignore bad habits, the harder they are to alter. Again, this is a strong argument for field coaching on a regular basis.

Fifteen bad work habits we should avoid in professional sales. Consider whether you do any of the following bad habits, jot them down, and start working on them. Think about whether you display any of the following bad habits; jot them down for reference.

1. **Beating yourself up:** This causes self-doubt and is close to rejection.
2. **Acting like a know-it-all:** You'll alienate your coworkers, and you might even provide misinformation to your customers. Know-all's are eventually disliked.
3. **Hoarding good ideas:** Refusing to offer assistance when your coworkers need advice, for example, sharing customer intelligence or helping another colleague.
4. **Avoiding prospecting:** The number one bad habit to fall into is not blocking off time for prospecting every week. I've been selling for many years, and I still set aside several hours each week for prospecting.
5. **Presenting too quickly:** One bad habit that will alienate your customer very fast is speaking or presenting too quickly.
6. **Skimping on research:** Planning and customer research is imperative prior to the first sales call; always show due diligence.
7. **Selling to everyone:** It is tempting to latch onto any lead that comes your way. But the time you spend on bad opportunities takes away from your capacity to pursue good ones. Only work leads that have a capacity of win-win.
8. **Lacking purpose:** Set goals for each day, week, month, and year you embark on, and be steadfast in meeting them. If you lack purpose, then the job is not for you.
9. **Whining and complaining:** Being a downer doesn't help your career, or anyone around you. When things feel bleak and every sales pitch is

a loss leader, it's tempting to wallow in your sorrows. Before you know it, negativity becomes a bad habit. Approach your day and its challenges with positivity, and learn something from the positive sales pros in your sales team. Be aware that whining salespeople do not last long.

10. **Watching "friends":** It's also important to network with other sales professionals in your city and sales team. Check LinkedIn or Meetup to find professional groups. Being a lone wolf is closing your mind to greater opportunities.

11. **Not walking the walk:** Roll up your sleeves and jump into your next call—no pretalk is necessary; just get on with the business of selling.

12. **Sitting all day:** This says to the sales manager you are not out there selling, simple.

13. **Writing too many e-mails:** Seeing your name published on the company blog will be good for your deals and for your career; look at the number of e-mails versus the number of sales calls you do.

14. **Not preparing enough:** I recommend that every salesperson prepare for his or her week on Sunday night (sorry to break up your weekend fun). It gives you an immediate plan of attack when you walk onto the sales floor on Monday morning. Please refer to the sales planning section for further advice.

15. **Giving up too soon:** This is my pet hate. People who give up because it gets too hard, shows a lack of determination. Never give up on a sale.

The bad habits list can go on forever in the personal, work-related, and sales domains. I have concentrated on the more prominent items to work on; next are the more annoying habits that customers find annoying too.[4]

Some of the minor bad habits to watch out for:

- Speaking too quickly, not articulating well.
- Be careful how you sit.

[4]Nine Bad Sales Habits Every Rep Should Avoid - James Meincke - January 3, 2019/I encourage all readers to study this important subject as we all inherit the bad selling habits.

- Don't fidget or play with your hair.
- Avoid clothing that may distract the customer's attention.
- Check your clothing outfit before going in for a sales call.
- Avoid carrying in too much hardware to make yourself look important.
- Speak clearly and watch for the customer reaction to your sentence.
- Do not speak over the customer when they are talking.
- Do not disagree with the customer under any circumstances.
- Agree with the customer when appropriate.
- Be very respectful to the customer.
- Do not overcompliment the customer.
- Do not boast about yourself; avoid showing family pictures unless asked for.
- Do not talk about yourself unless asked to, and make this brief.
- Do not go all out to make a friend out of your customer.
- Avoid talking about other competitors at all cost.
- Arrive at the sales site 10 minutes prior to the call to review strategy.
- Be on time always.
- If running late, call the customer, and do not text customer at all.
- If carrying sales information, present it in a professional manner; be well prepared.
- Avoid third-party references that are not qualified.
- Keep your phone technique short and to the point.
- Put your phone on silent mode when with the customer.
- Do not procrastinate; carry out all requested tasks.

Again, this list can go on for ages like the previous one, but the idea here is to highlight concepts you may be overlooking in your normal customer day.

How to Correct Small Bad Habits

The easiest and most effective way to correct the smaller and annoying bad habits is to ask a coach to ride with you for a day. I know this may seem ridiculous, but if you suspect you are annoying some customers, there is only one way to fix this: to have somebody work with you for a day and list all the small bad habits you make for correction. The second idea is to privately present a product on video and play it back; soon, you will recognize the habits in need of attention.

Is Procrastination the Number One Bad Habit?

If you need to change and want to change bad habits, you need to stop procrastinating now!

I would go so far as to say that most of us procrastinate in some way each week. "I will get around to it tomorrow or next week" or "it can wait." You are on the brink of making a critical personal change, and you find yourself delaying. The following shows how to apply the five phases of change to make priority changes.

But you know you are procrastinating and not getting the planning, research, and prospecting done. You are doing the day-to-day job of sales but procrastinating. To overcome procrastination and rectify this bad habit, please take note of the following.

Identify Why Procrastination Is a Problem

Question yourself. Is it fear of selling to new customers you are unfamiliar with, or are you just lazy? Are you unwell or just lacking in enthusiasm for the job? What is causing the lack of planning effort.

How to Plan and Schedule Your Week and to Prevent Procrastination from Proliferating

Here are some simple tasks to do – are you doing any of these?

- Sunday night, set weekly and monthly tasks to achieve. Put them down on paper.
- Put these tasks in the Outlook task menu so it reminds you each day.
- Set aside a half-day per week to make prospecting sales call appointments.
- Slide in sales calls on this appointing day only if they are urgent.
- Prospecting appointments can be scheduled into each week.

- Set aside how many prospecting sales calls per week you want to achieve.
- Set aside time for regional sales trips and time for appointing customers.
- Identify a product sales cycle for the prospecting sales call that will get you in.
- Make sure your sales manager knows you spend time at home or work appointing new business or, if the boss is sensitive about your being home, working from home; make a list of new customers, and do it during the day in the car.
- Stop looking at social media during the day.
- Avoid personal calls during the day.
- Have separate mobile phones for your private and professional needs.

This planning is not rocket science, and it doesn't take much to be organized. You will find this method refreshing and will be surprised how well you are organized. Just one warning: Don't get too comfortable at home; keep the job at hand organized and efficient. Stick to your plan and stay centered.

So, in a final review of how to make these simple but effective changes, try the following change program. What we are avoiding isn't the task but rather the stress that we are associating with the task.

Your Five-Phase Change Program to Consider

1. **Awareness:** Understand where it's coming from. A lot of people think that procrastination is just another word for laziness, but this isn't really true. It happens for all kinds of reasons, from perfectionism to stress and anxiety to unconscious thoughts that can leave you sabotaging yourself without even realizing what's happening. So if there's something that you keep putting off, ask yourself, "Where is this really coming from?" When you know what's at the root of the problem, then you can fix it. Avoiding awareness about you not being in the right zone means avoiding reality.

2. **Action: Fix any negative associations and procrastination—** Having negative associations with actions is one of the subtlest

but most common reasons for procrastination. For instance, if you have a negative association with making sales calls, then guess what? When it is time to make a sales call, you're suddenly going to find loads of other things that you "need" to do before you make the call. It is as if you go into a deep freeze and can't move on. I call this *Sales Freeze.*

The good news is that you can absolutely change your associations, even the really entrenched ones. You just need to create a new association with the action. Let's take the example of putting off your prospecting sales calls because you freeze up. Maybe you've been rejected on sales calls before, so you've begun to associate making prospecting sales with rejection. And then, working on that assumption, you've been timid and anxious on other sales calls, which has led to more rejection. This just reinforces the belief that making sales calls leads to rejection. See how it works?[5]

3. **Accommodation:** works through strategic planning (in other words, writing down a simple plan of attack as the one just laid out) and setting specific goals for the week, month, and year. Your boss will build these into sales KPIs, but sometimes these are related to sales achievements and training. It's about fitting in tasks that you can accommodate easily and that you can follow through without rejecting for practical and sensible reasons. Management of your tasks can be documented in Outlook easily.

4. **Acceptance and setting of a positive task outcome goal mindset:** The answer is to simply give this new process time to come together. Give the process at least 6 months as the prospecting sales calls will not show results for at least this long. This is accounting for the length of the product sales cycle of about 18 months.

5. **Actualization:** Setting weekly or monthly planning goals and getting over the customer appointing hump could just give you some sense of fulfillment, and you may appreciate you have some talent

---

[5]Procrastinating: how to stop it so you can sell more - By Anis 2018—Another paper worth reading as we all procrastinate in sales and wonder how to prevent this bad habit.

for this process. Once you have mastered this process and can show to your sales manager that you are on top of prospecting rather than procrastinating, you are well on the way to sales success. Making appointments by phone takes practice. Prepare a patter sheet and revise it accordingly. Have an experienced person sit with you, observing your success rate and voice modulation.

> The realization or fulfilment of one's talents and potentialities, especially considered as a drive or need present in everyone
>
> —Maslow's hierarchy of needs[6]

What Are Good Selling Habits?

The following good habits are just a few that successful salespeople do without thinking. Although they may not possess all these good habits, they generally show many of the following.

Good salespeople know how to make the product fit the customer's needs and take the lead to offer the right product for the need. They wait for the **customer's real** attention before starting the sale discussion and ask the right question to understand the customer's needs while engaging the prospect respectfully. They are not afraid of asking for the next appointment while on the first visit.

During sales calls, they take notes and then allow the customer to see that they are effective. They pass along opportunities when it's appropriate and have the ability to work closely with their sales team and sales manager. They take the initiative to assist their sales manager when requested within reason and are always happy to engage in further training and personal improvement. Show your boss that you may be keen to ascend the ladder.

This sounds easy, but after many of years selling, we should always be working on learning and including many more good habits in our daily work practice.

---

[6]Maslow's hierarchy of needs/Although very old as a reference, Maslow did publish an insight into the salesperson's hierarchy of needs.

How Can I Cultivate Good Habits and Be Mentally Strong?

This heading conveys the notion of mental toughness as having both reactive and proactive qualities. Mentally tough sales people can use mental toughness attributes to help endure and perform well during adverse sales situations, but they can also employ other attributes of mental toughness when the job is going well.

Mentally tough people make a habit of getting up after they have fallen down or pushing on after a sale has fallen through. Instead of getting upset, feeling hopeless, and giving up in the face of obstacles, they take the opportunity to put on their thinking caps and come up with a creative solution to the problem at hand. They are not discouraged when a sale does not go ahead but say, "Well, I will get the next one."

Losing a big sale is disappointing but understanding that this is part of the sales job helps balance out the wins and losses. Salespeople who lose a big or even a small sale and go to ground for a week would perhaps be better off finding another profession.

Some positive habits of mentally strong salespeople:

1. **They set real goals regularly:** Weaker salespeople don't think having their own personal goals will help them perform their jobs better. They are willing to let their companies set their goals for them in the form of strategic objectives and sales targets.
2. **They practice self-awareness:** They can tell when they are starting to get overexcited about an opportunity and make themselves relax and take it slow. Overexcited salespeople appear not to be in control and not to see the reality of their situation.
3. **They nurture a positive attitude:** When the selling process does not go their way, they do not give in to self-pity or seek solace from another colleague. Nurturing that positive attitude is the business driver that gets a strong salesperson back into the driver's seat in the face of setbacks, rejection, and obstacles. Again, the word determination creeps into the discussion.
4. **They commit themselves to constantly upgrading their business and sales customer education:** Disciplined learning strengthens the

mind, so strong salespersons read blogs, listen to podcasts, attend workshops, and get coaching from credible experts on things that relate both to the sales profession and to their industry. They have an innate attitude of continuous learning and do not block out criticisms that are valid. They learn from their mistakes and endeavor to fix these in an ongoing fashion.

In summary, having as many right habits as possible epitomizes the complete salesperson. We all know we are not perfect and carry with us habits that we are working on or seeking to work on. Stress less about this conundrum and just take each bad habit one by one, because this is a continual life process.

When Should I Seek Out a Mentor?

What Is a Sales Mentor as Opposed to a Sales Coach?

A coach is an expert on people and personal development, typically, a skilled sales specialist in competency or industry. A sales coach's role is to provide structure, foundation, and support so people can begin to self-generate the sales results they want on their own. Coaching is a process of inquiry, relying on the use of well-crafted questions, rather than continually sharing the answer, to get people to sharpen their own sales skills. Learning and growth are achieved by both parties involved in the coaching process.

The coaching relationship is built on trust and belief in the coaching method. It is always important for the coach to have industry experience first and have a TAE4101 coaching qualification in competency standards.[7]

Mentors—Professional and Nonprofessional

A mentor, on the other hand, can be internal for a salesperson, but I believe, as previously stated, the mentor should be independent and outside the industry. Usually, this is done on a professional level to advance the

---

[7]The benefits of mentoring new sales associates by ray Taylor on April 29, 2016—I like this reference as it underscores the need for a mentor position.

mentored person's career or by an older friend experienced with coaching and mentoring salespeople.

Often, mentors have their own approach already in mind and use the system that has worked for them in the past, without taking into consideration the style, values, integrity, or strengths of the people they mentor. As such, the mentor offers more solutions and answers to their mentee rather than questions that challenge people to change their thinking and behavior, thus making this more of a one-way, training-driven, rather than collaborative (coaching), relationship.

In the case of the procrastinator situation, who would be the better to consult, the coach or the mentor? Ideally, the coach, because he or she is more business-centric and has a handle on local and sales processes. The mentor, on the other hand, may certainly provide advice on a more global personal basis but not through a hands-on learning process.

As you can see, mentoring, in comparison with coaching, is a very different process, where one is active and the other consultative or passive.

How Do I Find a Mentor?

Once you are clear about the reason, identify who might help. For example, if you want advice on how to get to the next stage and access new networks and channels, join an industry association or network or try the following suggestions:

1. **The older sales colleague:** As with anything in life, if you don't ask, you don't get. And you'd be surprised at the number of people who'd be flattered to be considered "mentor material." Here, we are talking about another sales colleague that you get along with and have similar values that you respect; just ask as you have nothing to lose; if they say no, then go to the next one.

2. **Connection:** If you have a mutual connection, ask him or her to introduce you. And when you ask, make it clear exactly why you feel they'd be a good mentor for you and what kind of commitment you are seeking from them (a monthly coffee catch-up, the ability to run things past them via e-mail, or quick catch-ups via social media).

This is what you would call a loose arrangement but a semiformal request.

3. **Mentor programs**: Many industries have formal mentoring programs you can join. There are also wider mentoring programs on offer for "women in sales" or "small business" … and there are many online mentoring programs out there too. You only have to seek and "ye shall find."

4. **Mentor partnerships**: Look at ways to find a mentor outside of your sales field; someone of the opposite sex or an individual who has a different background than the one you have. Mentoring partnerships should not be limited to people who are similar to ourselves—there is a lot we can learn from people who are different than we are. This is particularly relevant if you are looking for advice on how to improve your sales skill set to suit a new industry.

5. **Online mentor:** Finally, you can ask for more formal mentors online and attend professional skill selling programs that include mentoring advice. Be aware that this costs money; also be aware of the upfront costs and consider whether it is for you. Remember, you get what you pay for.

My advice is to seek out an independent sales specialist mentor you can meet up with, say, every 2 weeks, for a coffee. Come prepared with any issues you need to discuss and follow their advice, simple and effective. Remember, you may have to pay for the service, but try it and assess the results after 6 months, it should be also tax deductible.

What Sales Courses Should I Take to Be a Better Salesperson?

This is a big subject to discuss and a great deal of information is available on the Net to look at and consider. This subject falls into three categories. First, does your current company provide sales courses, and does it have a field coach? Secondly, if you are not receiving sales coaching at work, what type of sales course should I target? Finally, at what level of sales experience are you now?

To assess the final question "at what level of sales experience are you at now?"

Try the Following Simple Test to Establish Your Current Experience in Sales

Selling Skills Assessment is a validated tool used to measure knowledge and ability in selling skills that have performance improvement potential. Complete the following five questions and cross the adjacent box.

Honest answers are imperative. *Be Honest Please!*

Buyer/Seller Relationships: How do you rate your buyer/selling relationship?

- ❏ Not good
- ❏ Fair
- ❏ Good
- ❏ Very good

Sales Call Planning: Rate your sales call planning and opportunity funnel health.

- ❏ Not good
- ❏ Fair
- ❏ Good
- ❏ Very good

Questioning/Listening: Do you actively practice customer probing for needs and listening.

- ❏ Not well
- ❏ Fair
- ❏ Good
- ❏ Very good

Presentation Skills: How are your presentation skills?

- ❏ Poor
- ❏ Good
- ❏ Very good
- ❏ Excellent

Gaining Commitment: What is your closing percentage now, and are you getting regular orders?

- ❏ Poor
- ❏ Good
- ❏ Very good
- ❏ Excellent

If your answers are *poor or below*, the situation is "serious to critical" and demands an answer to the question "do you enjoy sales, are you struggling with the selling concept, or have you not received any formal sales coaching?"

If your answers border on *good or below*, then it is time for a coach to help you to identify weaknesses in your personal skills. List these and try to understand where you need corrective tuition. Start with a list and work your way through it with your sales coach. Please give yourself a time limit of 3 months, no longer.

If you are in the *very good range*, then it is time to step up and improve along with further coaching, take specific courses that will improve your skills; keep at it, and don't give up.

If you have answered in the *excellent range*, you have either been self-deceptive or need to go back and retake the test "honestly." Alternatively, you may be in the excellent range and only need a tweak here or there; well done, but keep the improvement range high.

How Do I Find the Right Sales Course to Take?

First and foremost, don't take the first advertised sales course you see on the Net. Be guided by your style and what you personally want to start with.

Understanding the sales process and how to carry it out successfully

- Presentation skills in public
- Territory planning
- Efficiently use of time

These are just a few examples to consider. You will have, I guess, many more on your list, or you may not know what list to record in view of your lack of sales experience. If this is the case, ask a mentor or sales colleague to help you with a preliminary list. From this stage, short-list a group of RTOs that promote in-house basic sales training courses such as the Australian Institute of Management (AIM) or the main sales RTO's in the US and UK.

Speak to their course directors or promotion department and check them off against your needs list if they cover the subjects you need. You will find most basic sales courses are very similar, but the main question to ask is "is the course a competency-based sales course or partial sales product." What I am saying here is, are the course teachers qualified, and do they follow a logical sales program encompassing how the customer behaves?

I myself have personally completed many courses with AIM, in Australia, and many other sales and management courses worldwide. Start simple and work your way upward with the advice and support of your coach or mentor. As for the cost, try to have your company pick up the tab. If you show interest in improving your sales skills, your company should support you all the way unless your company is planning sales training themselves.

By the way, most accredited training courses are fully tax deductible in the majority of countries. Please remember that RTOs do not offer post-sales work in the field for individual students. This field training should be carried out by your sales manager or sales coach; however, if you have no access to a coach, then practice the following critique skills in the sales technique section of the next few chapters.[8]

---

[8]Sales Courses/Find your right fit online first. When looking for the right sales course, go online first and then ask your colleagues which courses they attended.

CHAPTER 11

Getting Down to Sales Technique and Planning

This chapter is comprehensive, with a great deal of detail relating to sales principles, such as whom to sell to, your opportunity CRM listings, closing fear, and the process of prospecting up to cold calling. Take it slowly with the information, and reread areas that may need further clarification.

What Are The Five Principles of Sales?

1. **Customers generally buy products and services that benefit them:** The first thing you need to know is that consumers don't buy from you because you're a great salesperson. It behooves you to accept and receive this truth in your business. Some companies have a "greater than God" attitude to selling their products and accept that they are empowered with this principle they follow. I call this

    believing in your own destiny

2. **Value comes with a price tag!** This principle is simple. The more your product or service benefits the consumer, the more you can raise the price. Some believe this philosophy, but in our competitive sales environment, companies that sell a "high-quality product" are brought back to reality when competitors have the same product and quality at a far cheaper price. We have seen this scenario play out with the introduction of Korean carmakers undermining the small Japanese car market at a very good price and long warranty cover. You see many companies follow this quality marketing principle, but in the long term they are confronted with global market reality.

This principle is held fast to by companies that sell a premium product and promote this concept, as, for example, the more expensive European carmakers. However, an examination of their product range shows that of late, they have been introducing a less expensive product in order to compete with their competitors. Is this product domination or competition pushing them in that direction? Even the best car made now has an SUV! So the answer, as we see this is, to offer a dual range, one cheap and the other expensive, sold under the premium brand.

3. **Credibility** is dependent on two factors—trust, expertise, and reliability. We develop this powerful, intangible quality of influence by cultivating the trust of our customers. This falls into two areas—personal credibility and company credibility. Your personal credibility is vital to your ongoing career and current sales situation. Without credibility *(Me Brand)*, you lose the customer's trust, and doubt enters the customer's mind. Moving on from this negative situation, recovering from the distrust situation, is near impossible.

4. **The most valuable gift you have to offer is yourself, your *Me Brand*.** As long as you're trying to be someone else, or putting on some act or behavior someone else taught you, you have minimized your opportunity. The most valuable skill in sales is yourself. Being natural and not making out you are somebody else is one of your most powerful tools. Trying to change your own personality to engage customers will be picked up by customer perception. Hiding yourself, to be another person, is deceitful and will be found out.

Persistence in Life and Sales

The best advice I can give to all new sales starters and existing salespeople is that dogged persistence is the key to achieving sales results. What I mean by persistence is not giving up in any circumstances. The best example of this is that if you were to lose a sale to a competitor, start the next day fully fresh and push on regardless. However, if you continue to lose sales, you may also need to review training, selling skills or your product you are offering the marketplace. You will find the great sellers of our time are patient, persistent, and always positive—**PPP.**

Attitude

You go "all in," with your head and your whole heart to provide the solution to a consumer's problem. This attitude is the fertile soil, where the trust the consumer gives you is nurtured and grows. In addition, you will feel great that you have solved a problem for your customer.

We are talking about being yourself, not trying to pull off somebody else and acting natural in the presence of other people. Never believe that the customer or client can't look into you and judge you. Do not underestimate the intelligence of our customers. In addition, your relationship with your company personnel and sales team is equally important.

BE YOURSELF!
So if you are about changing yourself, be yourself first!

Is My Company Helping Me or Not? True Story

Consider this situation. You have been working on a major sale worth US$500,000.

The sales cycle has been around 18 months, and you are at the quotation stage. Your customer has evaluated your offering and has given you excellent feedback on the product performance. Your company has been chosen over two other competitors to tender.

At the tender meeting, your key buyer has made it clear to submit *"only one price"* and indicated clearly that they will not be going through a negotiation stage for final selection.

You call a meeting with your sales manager and other management to discuss the tender offer and relay the customer's instructions of one price only. As the account manager, you put forward your recommended price to be offered and submitted.

Your company prepares the tender and sends it off for customer consideration without your consideration. Two months later, you receive an e-mail saying you have been unsuccessful for the tender. You follow up the reasons for the loss and are told your price was far too high and indicate to them that the offer was a starting offer, ignoring their full instructions. You relay the news to your boss and are asked, "Why did you not listen to me in the first place?" This scenario happens very commonly and indicates the lack of value management places on their people in the field.

This is the worst scenario to be caught up in. You go out of your way to work up a great deal that takes 18 months, many hours of work, and are blown away by ignorant and ineffective management that either disrespects your recommendations or are incompetent.

Sadly, this happened to me, and the deal was worth AU$850,000. Management did in the end acknowledge my recommendations, but they didn't listen!

Undertaking the Importance as a Salesperson

With all the responsibilities of the sales position, are we giving into management influence when you think you are right? The scenario says that I was neglectful in not being persistent in following up the final quotation going out. I recall I was very busy with many other installations going on at the same time and forgot the quote went out without my insistence on "one quote final only." I do take on this responsibility, but I didn't persist and push my management to do a first and final quote. Even at my age, you never stop learning.

Key Decision Makers in Sales

Who are these people, and which of them do I take seriously and whom do I ignore?

Key Decision Makers' Rating Scale

The following list breaks down who makes decisions and who can override any final decision.

V: Veto person can veto any decisions put to them
H: High decision maker
M: Moderate decision maker
L: Low decision maker
I: Influential decision maker
N: Not influential in any decision

My attitude is that any person with a stake in the use, operation, and function of your offering is important to convince.

When we analyze the preceding list, we notice that it describes the influence some of our customers wield. **N** is the customer that has no influence on decisions, but tread carefully with this person. They may have no decision making but they talk; they give their opinions to others that are key decision makers, so do not dismiss this person in the chain of command.

M: Moderate and low influence are again used as influences in the final product purchase. Although they have a lower rating of influence, they are asked in the final evaluation for their own opinion, and, collectively, their vote adds up considerably.

H: High decision makers are to be taken seriously. They are often in a purchasing position and are linked closely to the final Veto decision person. This person, or group of persons, often sits on a committee that decides the final recommendation of purchase that is passed to the board for approval and/or veto. Their decision process can be very complicated, such as purchasing, say, 20 anesthetic machines worth $1.5 million, or as simple as an additional set of power tools for the workshop.

V for Veto: The ultimate decision maker, end of the line, and the most difficult to gain access to.

The Veto person generally holds a position such as CEO, CFO, Director, or Department Director. Others are, for example, the Director for ICU, who has a great deal of pull, and his decision, depending on how respected it is, says a lot for the final decision maker.

Helpful Hint

To dismiss the high decision maker is akin to committing sales suicide. To overlook an N, no influence person, is to be an idiot.[1]

At the end of the day, the Veto person could up and change his or her mind against all the recommendations. Is there another agenda going on here? Some say yes, some say no.

---

[1]Identifying the five Key Decision Makers in the Sales Process/October 2018 by Zachary Cohen. A good author on this subject, he emphasizes the key decision makers as being critical to the sales process.

My personal experience says the Veto person is generally inaccessible to see and only listens to deals that give them and their company leverage. In a lot of cases, your management may play the game or not. From a global company perspective, your company may wish to "get into bed" with the ultimate buyer and reap the benefits; however, continued financial requests come thick and fast after the order goes in. The Veto person is generally an expert in financial manipulation in favor of their own business and will keep on exercising the business arrangement continually.

My message is this: Whether you are seeing the H, M, N, or V decision maker, see them all and tick off your notes into the project sheet and CRM; at least you will know more about who is the decider and who is not.

Suggestion

If you wish to influence the Veto decision maker over to your side, use your own managing director to meet up with the veto. This puts heads of companies in a much better leverage position and shows respect to the Veto person. Heads of private companies use every opportunity to do well for their organization. The deals that tend to go under the radar are doable only if your company ethics allow this kind of dealing.

Identifying funnel opportunities and how to prioritize.

What Is a Pipeline in Sales?

Every sales organization is limited in terms of how much effort and resources they can pour into closing each opportunity. Sales managers have only so many salespeople to work with, and salespeople have only so much time in a given day, week, month, or quarter.

It is therefore essential for managers to delineate an effective execution plan for tackling opportunities as part of their optimal sales pipeline management strategy; and a great part of this execution plan should focus on the prioritization of opportunities. The best sales managers rely on objective analysis to prioritize their sales pipeline opportunities and guide salespeople toward focusing on the most important or urgent sales to close.

We Call This Low-Hanging Fruit

The key to prioritizing sales pipeline opportunities is to find the right balance between level of engagement or effort and likelihood of closing, considering risk factors and the value of the opportunity and likely sales cycle time period. When we define the sale value, we are referring to the dollar amount up for closure and the value of the sales to product entrenchment and product brand expansion.[2]

Obviously, opportunities can't close unless they are being actively worked on by the sales team. Engagement could entail any number of different activities such as calls, e-mails, voice mails, productive connections, and product trials. Opportunities that display a low level of effort on the part of sales reps and haven't been engaged with in some time are less likely to close and should either be heavily focused on in a last-ditch effort to save the deal or purged from the pipeline as a dead opportunity altogether.

Purging an opportunity is completed from the funnel only if the opportunity is lost, not completed, or the customer has locked out the opportunity. Purging must be qualified face-to-face or confirmed by phone prior to deleting.

Suggestion

The assumption here is that the company is using a CRM software, and you are, like all others, using this tool as a major funnel and planning sales tool.

Opportunity Close Date and Forward Dating

Has this opportunity moved too frequently in recent times? Constantly shifting the close date forward could be an indication from the opportunity that they are not ready for your product now or that they are merely

---

[2]Pipeline research by Wendy Connick October 2017/Much has been posted on pipeline advancement and is a good reference to follow up on.

leading you along, with no serious intent to purchase. To justify this opportunity entry and to delete it, you must qualify the customer first in an honest discussion. Other date moves imply that the project has been delayed or that funding has been cut. In the end, you must find out the truth to decide the status of an opportunity. When I refer to truth, I mean your best hunch given the information you can collect.

The habit of forward dating or moving on an opportunity in CRM is being practiced all the time. What is of concern is the reason for forward posting the date of the opportunity and why.

Value

Is this opportunity worth significantly more (three times or greater) than your typical deal size? This should be a red flag. Typically, deals that are worth more tend to have smaller win rates and longer sales cycles, making deal size a *critical component of your sales pipeline.* These outliers should be carefully considered, not only when delegating opportunities (more experienced or successful salespeople should probably tackle these valuable opportunities) but also in forecasting sales. In addition, a large opportunity should be transferred to a project sheet form. Some companies say anything over US$250,000 should earn a project sheet automatically.

What Is a Sales Funnel?

Indifferent to a sales pipeline, the funnel represents the opportunities passing through the sales pipeline attaching close dates, description of product, service, and details appropriate to the opportunity. Sales funnel and pipelines service are a monitoring tool for management not only to assess sales potential but also to provide advance insurance for product need and build.

The following diagrams demonstrate two various sales funnels to understand. It is important to understand that all opportunities start at the top, outside of the funnel (the event horizon), and progress through verification to closure and order.

A Typical Sales Funnel

General Sales Funnel: 7 Steps

Generalized sales funnel that can be applied to any small business.

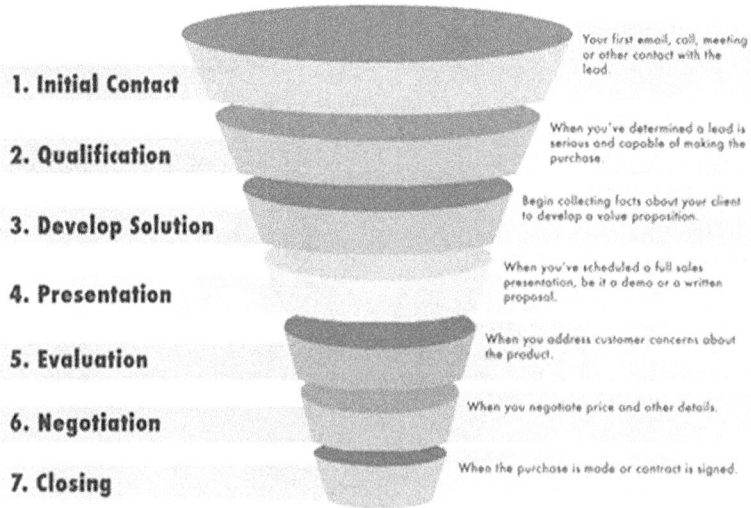

1. Initial Contact

Your first email, call, meeting or other contact with the lead.

2. Qualification

When you've determined a lead is serious and capable of making the purchase.

3. Develop Solution

Begin collecting facts about your client to develop a value proposition.

4. Presentation

When you've scheduled a full sales presentation, be it a demo or a written proposal.

5. Evaluation

When you address customer concerns about the product.

6. Negotiation

When you negotiate price and other details.

7. Closing

When the purchase is made or contract is signed.

FitSmallBusiness.com

Figure 11.1 A typical sales funnel to use
Note: The author acknowledges the use of this diagram, Fits Small Businesses.

Above the Funnel (the Event Horizon)

At this level above the funnel are many of your opportunities that are not yet qualified or sorted, in a hover situation. Frankly, I rate this area as the most important since the future opportunities end up as future sales. Sorting them by importance is vital so they take a place in the funnel.

What Are the Seven Steps through the Sales Funnel?

The sales funnel can be applied to any small business from the funnel opening down to the close of the opportunity sale.

1. **First contact with customer**: Engaging your first customer contact
2. **Qualification of opportunity**: When an opportunity becomes real, qualification status

3. **Develop solution for customer**: Offer solution to fit customer needs

4. **Presentation of solution**: Full demo/presentation of solution

5. **Evaluation and quotation**: Customer requests tender or quote

6. **Negotiation with customer**: Customer talks price

7. **Closing the sale**: The purchase order is received

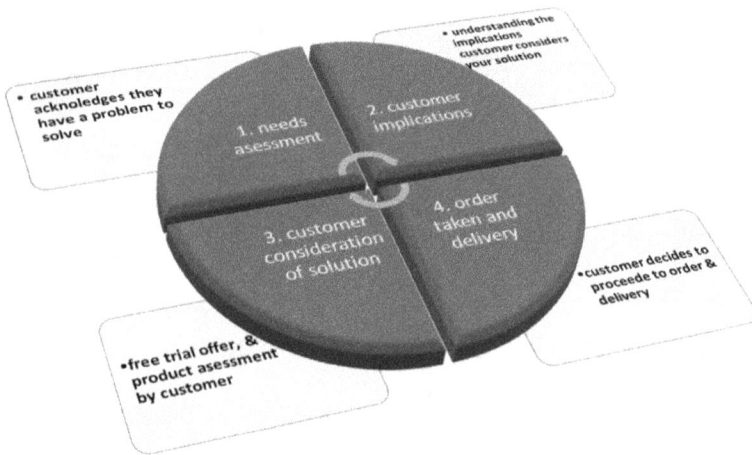

Figure 11.2 Customer engagement

So when you're thinking about the difference between a pipeline and a funnel, remember this: A pipeline report shows what a seller does during the sales process, and a funnel report shows the conversion steps through the sales process.[3]

Why Do Companies Place Such Importance on the Sales Funnel?

It comes down to an internal company process developed over many decades. When you consider the system used in the nineties for sales printouts and the enormousness of the paper put in front of you, the process now becomes much more meaningful and easier to understand. The other

[3]What is a Sales Funnel, Examples and How to Create One (Guide) Home Analytics Last Updated on January 15, 2019?

reason is that management can review, assess, and predict better sales forecasts generally 18 months out with reasonable accuracy. Finally, manufacturing can predict and forecast future materials and product needs.

For you as a salesperson, you have a ready-made system at your fingertips waiting to be updated and reviewed. This process is imperative to keep up to date.

Weekly/Monthly/Quarter and Yearly Sales Activity Reports

First, the weekly sales activity report will go to sales management generally by Monday morning for review. This report is independent of the CRM pages produced. Sales reports generally show the following information:

- Sales for the week.
- Sales against weekly budget in a unit plus percentage.
- Product groups may be split up and produced in separate increase versus previous months.
- Sales reports will include monthly, quarterly, and yearly sales to date results.
- More detailed reports will show sales results against CRM funnel opportunities.

Be aware that some companies will not register your sale to your territory until delivery is enacted and signed off by the customer. This is ever important in the medical capital arena since some large installations entail a long complicated installing process.

The list can go on and become even more complicated with the slicing and dicing of results. All you need to know, as a sales person, is what monthly sales budget you need to achieve, how you can get this result through funnel opportunities that mature into close, and what sales are coming up for the next few months.

It does get a bit sensitive when you are perhaps only 60 percent of the sales plan by end of November and you only have one more month to close business, given that delivery may take 6 -8 weeks. If you follow the review process ahead of your current sales at hand, you should be driving the closing deals early before November and cleaning up in December, ready for the start of the new year, given that your company works on a calendar year.

Strategic Sales Project Sheets

Project sheets are great to use and can be a valuable part of analysis for the sales team to bring in other assistance. Project sheets demonstrate the scale of the project and the number of participants needed to execute the final order. Project sheets come in various styles and can be as simple as a one-sheet project form. The information of a project sheet should show

- Size of project
- Product offering or group of product/service offerings
- Total dollar sales worth
- Bring together sales team participation
- Bring together sales management cooperation
- Force accountability of all working parties
- Coordinate dates of task completion
- Ensure a winning offer
- Anticipated close of the project details in dates
- Customer details
- Company people involved
- Key players

I have used many project sheets from the ad hoc to global prepared software strategic analysis sheets linked into CRM. Believe me, they all work as long as the parties involved are contributing to their designated tasks and delivering the results on time.

Some of the Details Needed for a Comprehensive "Project Sheet"

Strategic project sheets provide visibility into sales opportunities, documenting plans with the program's project sheet. This involves identifying all key players in the customer's organization, understanding each player's degree of influence and their reasons for buying, and uncovering essential information. Salespeople and organizations will be equipped to evaluate their competitive position, address the business and personal motives of each decision maker in the client organization, and differentiate their company by leveraging its unique strengths.

Strategic selling significantly improves the odds of winning complex sales opportunities. It gives organizations a common process and language for pursuing sales opportunities and criteria for allocating resources to determine when to walk away from resource-intensive deals with low probabilities of success. Date, closing date, objective, overall components of the plan, direction of flow, deliverables, and who, how, and when are just some of the details you need to record on the project sheet.

What is interesting is that when tasks for the forward progress of the project and allocation of tasks have been agreed upon, it is very interesting at the next project sheet meeting to uncover who has not completed his or her allocated task. Ever more so when your sales manager has not completed his or her task! This process forces accountability and also exposes the one who has not seen the KDMs, key decision makers, of your project. Finally, it is important that you, the owner of the project, contribute equally and drive the project to its conclusion. You must take responsibility and full control here, so be strong and determined to complete your project. As the project sheet leader, you are ultimately in charge.[4]

Customer Buying Cycle

How important is it to understand the customer buying cycle, and can we be confident the cycle is relevant today? My personal opinion is that buying cycles differ according to what type of industry you are selling in. The variations come in retail sales, vehicle sales, housing sales, food and wine sales, luxury goods, and so on. These buying cycles are not only variable but seasonal too. When an economy goes into decline, we see a drop of retail, and luxury items go on the back burner. In the medical business sector, I have seen seasonal buying play a role and fiscal influence determining ordering pattern change. Ordering in January is generally slow for obvious reasons, and June is the same, but when governments release funding for hospitals in July to September, we see peaks in orders.

---

[4]Blue Sheets – Not Just for the "Sales" Department/12/02/17—This paper is an honest assessment of project sheets and their place in sales.

Buying cycles are also interrupted by specific customer need. One-off or, for example, a generator going down and the hospital needing a replacement urgently changes the routine of the cycle.

The Customer Buying Cycle in General

Figure 11.3 The customer buying cycle process

As a very simplistic description of a customer buying cycle, the diagram shows the process as the customer progresses through the four buying stages. In retail buying, the process happens fast, but in, say, capital sales, the process could take up to 2 years from start to order. The four steps (free trial or evaluation) could be the longest process. Evaluation trials could take up to 12 months to complete.

Customer and Your Behavior during the Sales Call

As you begin your selling career, it is important to ask yourself the following questions so you can do a quick assessment on how you perceive customers.

1. Do you see the company's side first and neglect the customers?
2. Do you think the customer is always wrong or right?
3. Are you too close to your customer so your judgement is clouded?

4. Do you see the customer's vision?
5. Are you willing to go the extra mile for your customer?
6. Are you able to see your customer's needs?
7. Are you able to deal with your customer's problems and issues?
8. When quoting, do you give too much discount to favorite customers?
9. Are you uncomfortable to ask for the order (closure phobia)?
10. Are you able to conduct a post sales call critique?
11. Do you understand the seven critical steps of the sale?
12. Do you treat the customer as a real person?

It is very important to answer these questions honestly. If, for instance, you answer questions 4, 5, 9, and 10 negatively, then there is a need to get with your mentor and discuss the results of this questionnaire.

If you are suffering from several phobias that restrict you from functioning as a professional sales person, then seek help in the field. Having a phobia or fear of closing or asking for the order is common, but, unfortunately, this is a key function of selling; get help please.

Put Yourself in the Customer's Position, and Consider How They See You

The questions below dig a little deeper to uncover how the customer views you and the things you do to earn customer respect.

- Are you a good listener and show this skill?
- Do you avoid wasting time?
- Are you prepared with valid selling tools?
- How do you show respect to your customer?
- How do you show you are attentive to your customer?
- Do you promise and not follow through?
- Do you undermine your competitors?
- Do you use third-party references without checking first?
- Do you look at your presentation, including your dress code?

Remember that the name of the game is for you to return to your customer many times in the future. The evidence shows that revisiting your customer on a regular basis is an excellent way to develop a lasting sales relationship that leads to sales.

Closing Order Phobia

Phobias are irrational anxieties. Salespeople can be overly fearful of closing a sale. Closing phobia is surprisingly common. Watching salespeople try to close a sale and ask for the order when the person suffers from a phobia is devastating for the coach and the person concerned. Fortunately, there are effective ways to overcome this devastating problem. Firstly, let's look at the closing phobia and why it happens.

Symptoms of Sales Closing Phobia Are

The main symptoms are, anxiety, sweaty hands, willing to cancel the sales call, increased heart rate and a complete feeling of fear.

Consequences If This Were to Happen?

Consider what it would mean if you never made a sale again. Some terrible scenarios might include getting a job that doesn't involve sales at all, hiring a salesperson for your business, or getting outside help to improve your sales technique. When you follow through on your fears and imagine the worst-case consequences, you'll see that they're not nearly as catastrophic as you imagine.

One of the most common challenges facing people trying to make a sale is the fear of rejection and the consistent fear and uncertainty of knowing when to ask for the order. The following are some of the signs that show that the potential for rejection is crippling you:

Your Focus Is on the Possible Rejection

You have one major question at the back of your mind: "What if they say no or I will think about it a little?" You're not thinking about more critical concerns, such as "Is the client a good match for your target market? What can I help them with?"

Every Rejection Feels Like a Sign of Failure

You usually feel like rejections are a sign that you're not good at your business or that your product or service isn't good enough. You also feel this way even when customers are merely unresponsive or defer their buying decisions.

You Take Days to Recover from Rejection

Whenever a lead doesn't want to take your offer, it's at the back of your mind for more than a day. It's possible you even replay the interaction to see what you could have said or done to close the sale. You might even feel some bitterness toward the person or sales in general.[5]

These are just a few of the symptoms many of us have in regard to asking for the order. The opposite is the salesperson that never stops asking for the order. This person seems to be far removed from the conversation going on during the sale but thinks, "I'd better ask for the order anyway. I myself suffered for a few years from closing phobia."

How Do I Get Past the Fear of Rejection?

Think about the type of person you'd be if you didn't have this fear. Include everything from what you'll be feeling internally, how you'll carry yourself, and what you'll do to prepare for the sales task. Note also how your body responds to the idea of sales. For example, if you get sweaty and feel butterflies in your stomach when trying to make a sale, think about how you'll react instead if you weren't afraid. While this won't eliminate your fear responses, you'll at least have an idea of what your next action should be and how you should carry yourself despite your fear.

How to Overcome Fear in Closing the Sale

When the fear is too much, list some small wins you can accomplish more easily. These small wins don't have to be sales tasks, but they should

---

[5]How to Overcome Fear of Selling, May 30 2012 by Susan Martin/Martin explains the sheer fear for some that suffer from such a phobia and how to deal with it effectively. Four Things Mentally Strong Salespeople Do That Average Reps Don't.

be relevant to customer acquisition or lead nurturing. Going for easer or low-hanging fruit bolsters your closing confidence and gives you the enthusiasm to push up for more difficult closing situations.

Recognizing Closing Fear and General Anxiety

The fear generally follows the same symptoms of severe to moderate anxiety. You will feel the following.

- Excessive worrying about all things
- Agitation
- Being very restless
- Suffering from fatigue
- Avoidance of exercise
- Lack of concentration
- Being irritable
- Muscular tenseness of chest and shoulder area
- Trouble sleeping
- Having panic attacks
- Avoidance of being with people
- Irritability

Many of the items on the preceding list fall into classic anxiety, playing out into closing phobia and the fear of rejection.

Helpful Hints to Reduce the Fear and Anxiety in Selling and Closing

- **Upload some new content into your business'** social media pages. Anything short will do, as long as it fits the voice of your brand, such as links to an article, a link to a specific product page on your site, an inspirational quote, or a fun GIF (graphics interchange format).
- **Optimize your social media pages,** if you haven't done it yet.
- **Respond to messages** from potential customers who are asking for more information about your products or service. Give them

the information they need (no need to overtly sell), then follow up with a face-to-face sales call.

- **Read a chapter of a book** related to entrepreneurship, sales, marketing, or your industry.
- **Find ways to improve the product pages** of one or two products or services on your site. Use one or more of these psychological triggers for inspiration.
- **Prior to the sales call**, think of positive results and past wins.
- **Practice breathing** prior to and during the sales call.
- **Get excited** about a new sales possibility.

Most importantly, before asking for the order, put yourself onto another mental plane. Mentally detach yourself from the current reality and see the meeting from above. Ask for the order and step back; do not continue to talk and wait for the reply. If it is rejected, then be prepared to fight on another day. By putting yourself into another space, you will feel protected and will not take it seriously. Remember the best sellers loose some sales too.

Don't take rejection to heart: You are in business, and there will always be sales you can't achieve. So, accept that you will win some and lose some. Stop stressing over this, and get on with the business of sales. Additional things to do:

Set a regular time every day for 30 minutes to exercise.

See a doctor to discuss the problem and some treatment if needed.

Mentor, discuss the problem, and work out a feasible action plan. If the problem continues and seems impossible to overcome,

Stop–Assess–Plan–Review–Accept Help–Try to Overcome–Practice[6,7]

I too suffered from rejection, and I firmly believe every new sales person shares the same fear. Practicing the above strategy over a period will build your confidence, so asking for the order will not work unless you are more

---

[6]Nine ways to overcome fear of rejection in sales/I fully recommend this article.

[7]Australian Research.

than, say, 80 percent sure you will get it. If you are unsure of getting a yes, then keep probing for objections and positive answers. You will overcome this with positive thoughts and persistence. Believe me, it works!

If Your Customer Says No

When you ask for the order and the customer say's no, there is a very good reason for this answer. There is no harm in asking why. You have not lost anything so ask why and then you know where you stand and what the next move should be. Just so I am clear why you wish to not go ahead with the order, may I ask why please" you should get an honest response.

Being Too Pushy

To be pushy in sales is being arrogant and disrespectful to the customer. Being pushy in business is sometimes considered as driving to be successful too quickly. Being pushy is also associated with not giving anybody around you recognition that their feelings and ideas count at all. Finally, the individual needs to recognize the need to stop being pushy and to seek intensive coaching. In the end, it is an inherent or deliberate persona an individual portrays as a method of getting what he or she wants.

To overcome the fear of being pushy requires you to dig deep. Sometimes, we think of sales as something manipulative or sleazy because we often think it's coming from a place of dishonesty. While there are certainly unscrupulous people trying to make a quick buck, the fact that this makes you feel bad means that you aren't likely to be one of those people. The pushy salesperson will have some success as some customers will cave in to the pressure.

Taking Ownership

There are two types of salespeople, those who do not take ownership and those that do. Have a look at the following list and see which sentence applies to your ownership style.

- You know your personal limitations.
- You have a clear single sales objective prior to the sales call.

- You treat your territory as your own business.
- You show leadership in your patch.
- You learn from your mistakes.
- You build trust with all sales and business members.
- You are a good team member.
- You think outside the square.
- You thank people who assist you.

The preceding list touches on the more personal items we need to check prior to selling. The more you take ownership, the more respect you receive and the more people are willing to help you. Taking ownership of your territory shows your manager you own everything going on within. This, in turn, provides your manager with a degree of confidence that you are managing your business well and competently. There is no course you can take to learn ownership. It comes from within and shows pride and keenness on being the manager of your patch.

Ultimately, taking ownership is showing a high degree of pride and responsibility for your sales area.

Territory Planning, Guide, Techniques, and Suggestions

Of all the territory functions one has to perform, territory planning seems to be the most difficult to carry out. Acknowledging that territory planning requires an organized mind, there is a specific system you can learn to become effective. In my career, I have not met a coach or trainer that had a logical and specific method of teaching territory planning. This is a big statement, but most, if not all, salespeople I have taught need and want to know how to plan the territory effectively. It almost falls into the area of mystique, and salespeople need to master the holy grail of planning.

My method is proven, simple, and easy to follow.

What You Need to Do First

You must commit to being an organized person and always have a medium- to long-term goal. Develop a strategy for each day and week, jot this down, and post it on a wall. Utilize your CRM opportunities, and prioritize the low-hanging fruit. Set aside time every week to review opportunities and appoint new business, and review where your customers are and delineate metro from country accounts.

For larger accounts, plan visits together with multiple accounts to save time; also learn how to use CRM and Outlook well, and use a reminder "to do" folder within. Finally, utilize Sunday nights to start with, so the week starts clear of planning needs. With larger opportunities or projects, set up a project sheet meeting to call in company personnel to work with.

Territory Planning Starts with Paper and Pencil and a Willingness to Prospect for Sales

This is a go-to list for planning. If you are missing some of the suggestions, try to include them in your week. Remember that encouraging others to help you is great, but understand that they too have a job. For the nuts and bolts of how to get territory planning activated, read on further.

Prospecting for New Business—Time Involved

Prospecting should be around one-third of your week's activity. Calling and servicing your current client base is imperative, and new business comes from this activity. If you go weeks without any prospecting activity, it will set you back months and create a huge gap in the future sales and opportunity pipeline. Actively prospecting new customers and opportunities secures a healthy funnel and removes the opportunity gaps. When the gap in opportunities comes around, you wake up one morning with "no" work on.

Remember, many sales managers and coaches do not know how to teach territory planning effectively. This statement was clearly reported in the research.

A healthy funnel would be going out farther than 18 months and should include short-term opportunities closing in 2 weeks, opportunities in the medium and long term.[8]

---

[8]Prospecting the future. A reference that shows other ways of prospecting and reinforces the importance of this sales function.

How Do I Start a Prospecting Planning Method?

This method assumes you have just started in a new sales position, job, or territory.

- Plan allocated time each week for active prospecting appointing. The following weeks' activities should be full, with provision made for emergencies.
- In most cases (depending on distances), plan for a minimum of five appointments per day.
- Classify your customers into A, B, C according to past sales records.
- A customer is your best buyer, B customer is a lower but important buyer and C customer is and opportunity buyer or customer that has not purchases whatsoever.
- Plot on a map your territory and where your customers exist if you are unsure.
- Review distances between customers for background knowledge.
- Carry out a diary cleanup, providing ample time for driving and review between sales calls. Always leave ample time to arrive and review *your* sales strategies prior to your customer meeting.
- Review and appoint metro versus country sales trips with a balance of 25 percent for country visits and 75 percent of sales calls in metropolitan areas. Please note that visits to the country should be booked on a regular basis and not a six-monthly turn up because you had a gap in your diary; regular attention to country customers pays dividends.
- Prospecting activities should take you out 2 months ahead. This is because appointments made more than 3 months ahead always change or are canceled.
- Reconfirm long appointments just prior to the sales calls.
- Review your task notes to include in this planning system.
- When in the country, plan driving times from account to account.
- It is important to see all customers in your territory so as to assess potential sales and any past problems unresolved.
- Appoint the first 2 weeks and then progress with the weekly method thereafter.
- For the first 2 months, appoint "all customers," not half for the start.

Your manager may say leave the C- and some B-class customers for later. What your sales manager is saying is "I want sales now."

To begin to prospect gathering, keep an objective mind. If the prospect is given to you by a third party, first qualify validity, business existence, and local knowledge; in other words, ask around. You may without qualification make an appointment and continue with the sales call, wasting valuable time and resources. Always be shrewd about every prospect given to you by another party. Qualify first!

Appointing Techniques for Beginners

Appointing over the phone when you do not know the customer is daunting. The customer will take into consideration your company name and reputation, how you approach them over the phone, and when you are able to visit or when the customer is available. Also, the tone of your voice is vital. Being overly respectful or gushy is not cool these days; be natural.

These are some examples of appointing approaches: at all costs, avoid being cheesy.

> *"Hi Susan, my name is .... I represent ...., and I would appreciate some of your valuable time to introduce myself and find out a little more about your department needs please."*

> *"Hi Susan, my name is ...., I represent ...., and would love to catch up with you next week regarding your transport truck fleet used in Dallas and what current challenges you have."*

> *"Hi Susan, my name is......................, I represent ...., I would appreciate some time with you next week to talk about your department's patient monitoring needs and, if time permits, to introduce our new monitoring systems."*

> *"Hi Susan, my name is ...., and I represent ...., a colleague or yours; Dale Smith recommended I give you a call to touch base regarding your new office renovations project for next year."*

> *"Hi Susan, my name is.............., and I represent ...., I have replaced {last rep name}, and I would appreciate visiting you to establish contact with your department, please?"*

There are no assumptions built in. Be respectful and introduce yourself first. Take a big breath before calling, and have an objective. Try not to be specific unless asked first, and be flexible around the customer's time schedule. These techniques always work because you are courteous and respectful.

Why Is It So Difficult to Secure a Second Appointment?

If your meeting goes very well, you tend to forget to ask if you can visit again when you are in town next.

This is one of the key failings of salespeople, and you are then required to call back and obtain the customer's authority to meet up soon. I am not referring to "cold calling." I am not against cold calling but only in very select situations. The technique is simple, and there is no follow-up required. Just as you leave, ask, "by the way, may I visit you again when I am in town next, please?" Your customer will, in most cases, agree. Next time you call or e-mail for an appointment, they will recall their previous commitment.

Unless the customer is expecting some further information from you, he or she is not expecting to see you on a regular basis. It is up to you to initiate this permission. Alternatively, if there is no opportunity foreseen, just ask, "Could I keep in touch with you from time to time or send you new product updates?"

Always ask for the customer's business card, and seek permission to keep in touch through e-mail. We call this a "foot in the door." There is nothing wrong with this technique, and if you don't do this, your competitor will.

Follow-Up Second Sales Call, What to Do and Include

I have been challenged many times. If a customer asks for a quote, I send it by e-mail, and then I drop a copy plus brochure in personally. I am criticized for what is seen as over servicing. Absolutely not! It keeps your face in your customer's face and demonstrates you are active in your territory. The second call may give you the opportunity to answer any customer questions they may have. It is smart selling. Don't listen to the doubters, deliver the quote in writing as a cold call and you will see the magic of what happens.

Always include a quote promised to the customer in a hard copy folder.

After following any customer needs, progress to a product demonstration. Make sure you have plenty to talk about, and listen carefully to customer needs to react in the right way. Utilize CRM notes to follow up on what strategy is next.

Pros and Cons of Cold Calls

Cold calling used to be one of the best—and only—prospecting strategies salespeople could use. But in the past 40 years, a range of more effective alternatives have emerged.

- **Consistent:** It reliably generates new leads, according to the older establishment of sales professionals, but find a customer who has plenty of time to receive cold calls these days! In fact, it's fair to say that anyone interrupting your day with an uninvited 3-minute patter is going to have to do some seriously fast and impressive talking to keep you on the line. Let's face it, the odds aren't on the salesperson's side, so why bother cold calling at all.
- Chances are that the caller has already had to get creative about how they got through to your office in the first place, and the sales call itself has probably begun with you being mildly irritated at best.
- This practice is based on opportunistic behavior and a lack of real planning. Other sales trainers call this "see more numbers of customers to gain more sales."

Yes, seeing more numbers is the name of the game, but what about quality sales calls?[9]

There is an upside to playing the numbers of additional sales calls, but when you analyze the actual hit rate and the numbers of orders that come from cold calling, you will find it sadly low. Customers see this as

---

[9]200+ Sales Statistics You Must Know [Real data for 2019 & beyond and ideal analysis of sales statistics]

a lack of respect and an avoidance of making a proper appointment. The likelihood of getting to see a customer is slim unless you know his or her work movements well.[10]

The only time cold calls should be utilized is when you are working near a customer; try it, but don't make a habit of this practice; you must be sensitive to this practice.

Territory Planning in Summary

Haplessly trolling your territory is inefficient; avoids targeting the low-hanging fruit; and says you are not interested in short-, medium-, and long-term sales. It is primarily an unscrupulous way to operate. Territory planning takes discipline and commitment to put down a plan that reflects regional and metro appointments matched to your sales funnel.

I was asked numerous times how to do territory planning as a coach. I came up with a process (covered in this chapter) that produced excellent sales results, with a healthy funnel that panned out at least 18 months.

You may disagree with my technique, and your sales manager may also claim to have a better method. What management wants you to do is make customer appointments on the run and not take time off for appointing. I understand that from a manager's perspective, but planning appointments with your funnel in mind takes concentration and thought, and this is not completed effectively on an ad hoc basis.

Your manager essentially does not want to hear about how much time you spent in the car or home office appointing opportunities; he only wants to see "sales." So, you take the choice to inform or not to inform. When he/she calls you and you say you are at home appointing, immediately they will think negative thoughts. Don't let this bother you. Do your job and get on with appointing business; end of story. The business in the end is judged by continuous sales and appointing is just the process we do.

---

[10]The *Harvard Business Review* reported *cold calling is ineffective 90 percent of the time,* and more recent research shows that less than 2 percent of cold calls actually result in a meeting. Assuming a 0.3% appointment-booking rate and a 20 percent win rate, it would take *6,264 cold calls to make just four sales.*

CHAPTER 12

Overview of Learning the Great Skill to Sell—The Fun Part

For New sales People, Experienced Sales People, Sales Managers and Sales Coaches

Now let's get down to the final sales skill: "selling."

Every business has to sell in order to survive, and not everyone understands how selling is a way of encouraging the customer to achieve what he or she needs. This chapter will introduce you to the principles of selling in a way that removes the fears that new or existing salespeople have. The key factor is to be open to learning new ways of selling and be willing to accept critique until you are up and skilled.

We have discussed through the book various methods proposed by RTOs and internal coaching systems. Here, I will present a seven-step simple selling approach that is easy to follow and understand. The main takeaway is that during the sales call, you should know, with some practice, where you are on the seven steps and how to get back on focus to complete the sale.

You may be sitting next to an experienced sales person in a Monday sales meeting, but this person may not be able to classify or repeat the 7 steps of the sale process. They probably just sell on auto pilot. I was one of these till I had an interest on how the process worked.

Who Will Benefit from This Chapter?

Those new to selling who are required to promote their organization and sell their products and services and those who need to understand the correct way to sell honestly and ethically. The chapter also delivers skills learning to sales managers and sales field coaches. You are never too old to learn the best way to sell to your customers, and this includes professional salespeople too.

Admission of Guilt—Time for Honesty

For years as a new sales person, I didn't know the steps of the sale. I was never taught or given tuition on this very important subject. The Internet was not available, and companies were deficient in this coaching task; they just expected you to know. As time went on, you just forgot to learn the basic sales steps and got on with selling, or what you thought was selling; I call it **"selling on autopilot."**

I would go so far as to say that 85 percent of professional salespeople out there cannot recite the full seven steps of the general sales process. For instance, I have found most sales managers can recite at least three to four steps but can't clearly write down the seven steps as they themselves have not studied this process.

If, however, your sales manager or sales coach is unable to recite the seven sales steps, you may have a problem. During my coaching career, I did this simple test at the beginning of each sales course. Not one could recite the seven steps except a customer service person I worked with, and to my astonishment, she recited the seven steps backward! The group was amazed.

Is there any benefit of knowing this simple seven-step sales process? Some would say it is not on the high priority list, but I would argue otherwise. Going back to where I started off in sales, I now wish I had this information to study at the time.

What Will You Get Out of Learning a New Sales Technique?

Understanding a simple seven-step process of ethical sales and what to do next and how to gain the customer's **"real"** attention—GFA.

Gaining Favorable Attention

Gaining attention and respect from your customers as a salesperson specialist and developing a role as a professional salesperson and product advisor.

When you first meet a new or existing customer, do the respectful greeting and wait for their response. Do not proceed with the sale until you have the full attention of the customer. They will have distractions such as email, intercom, phone and other people entering their office. Wait till you are convinced you have GFA.

Learn how to listen to your customer's needs and provide solutions to overcome the customer's problems; applying sales techniques that build rather than destroy relationships along with presenting the features and benefits of the solution and knowing how to present the solution.

How to gain the customer's commitment to buy along with closing the sale and following through to ensure customer satisfaction; finally, how to conduct post-sales call self-critique analysis and the further use of customer relationship management (CRM) in support of prospecting sales.

Learning Outcomes for Ethical Sales

1. Participants should be able to understand and accept the benefits of working in an ethical sales-oriented culture in a global organization.
2. Support selling as a positive behavior for meeting customer needs.
3. Be able to use nonmanipulative sales techniques (ethical selling).
4. Finally, use features and benefits correctly to demonstrate their solutions and to promote products and services based on value rather than price.

In the end, if you apply the ideas presented, your success rate will improve over a six-month period. The proviso is that you apply an attitude of continual learning and self-analysis. In addition, you need to adopt a mentor and use your sales manager or field coach to assist you to improve.

Helpful hints: consider a few of the following preliminary suggestions:

- Never take your eyes off your customer; maintain complete focus during the sale.

- Keep to your SSO, or single sales objective.
- Do not be distracted by the ringing of your mobile phone; turn it off.
- Work on the customer relationship for several minutes, keeping this to a minimum.
- Establish the customer needs while assessing what you can offer instead.
- Do not assume anything during probing, summary, and closing.
- Maintain the seven-step sales process to keep on track.
- Customer follow-up should be completed and sent within 24 hours.
- Always ask to return again.
- Be positive, professional, and persistent.

Follow the very simple seven steps of the sale[1]:

1. Meeting Plan
2. Customer Appointment and First Meeting—GFA
3. Needs Establishment
4. Demo – Presentation
5. Overcome Objections
6. Summary— Commitment
7. Close or Advance to Next Stage

The following seven steps of the sale are your cornerstone for ethical and professional sales technique; practice this method

1. Reason for sales call, utilize background customer information, come up with an SSO. Don't visit the customer to meet and greet only, but have a sales objective for the visit.
2. Gaining favorable attention is vital. In the first meeting, you will spend more time chatting and developing a rapport. Time to

---

[1]Teaching Sales/Suzanne Fogel, David Hoffmeister, Richard Rocco, Daniel P. Strunk/ Harvard Business Review/An insight into the need for trained and qualified sales coaches. Runs along the same lines as my thoughts.

establish customer positioning and summing up what potential is there for business.

3. Using probing questions of customer needs, you should be able to position your product to meet needs. Needs payoff can be established at this stage also.

4. Performing a product demo or presentation will solidify and bring together customer need resolution. There will be some questions and objections to answer, time to prepare your mind for the next step.

5. When objections come up, it is imperative to answer them objectively and accurately with the view that the customer sees them as solving their problem. If you are unable to answer a question, commit to providing the answer as soon as possible.

6. When you feel the sales call has progressed enough, summarize, incorporating need resolution, product offering, and any other feature and benefit required. If when the six steps have progressed suitably and you are comfortable to close, ask the question for close.

7. "Closing fear" appears at this point as you have not covered off objections correctly or you have totally missed your customer's needs or aspirations. In addition, prework may not have been effective enough to uncover as much information as possible. Closing is only left for the point where you feel very satisfied your customer has traveled the process with buying signs and you consider the customer sees your solution and is saying yes to moving forward.

GFA—Gaining Favorable Attention of Your Customer

The seven steps will not proceed without any customer attention. Many sales managers consider this stage to be trivial and accept that they always get the attention of the customer. Personally, this step is the most important part of the sale. Research tells us that a customer will or will not like you within the first 60 seconds of meeting. A customer will consider during this very short period of time, whether they will let you continue and listen to you. If you miss this vital point of eye and body language contact, you have totally missed the first sign.

Observe the office, wall items, desk items, photos to connect with the customer first. This observation is essential to gauge the customer's personality. Commit these physical items to memory for future sales calls.

Items You Will Need to Be Alert to and Aware of—Drilling Down Further

What information do you need regarding strategy, that is, what will you need to take into the sales call? Props, references, brochures, laptop, or tablet. Avoid taking in heavy overweight bags and briefcases. Ultimately, an iPad will suffice. Bags and luggage distract the customer.

Explore the customer situation, any business issues to talk about, challenges they have, and problems. Are there decision makers above the customer, or is the customer the key decision maker? Be sure your product will impact on their performance and when they are buying and how many. Timelines become important in the sales close.

Select the solution for your customer—needs-based selling While exploring the customer's needs, be careful not to jump prematurely into your offer or solution. This can be a big trap, and you may end up running off course without realizing you have. If you offer your product/ service solution, be very sure that it is going to solve the customer's needs!

In your own mind, formulate your specific product/service offer and proceed to introduce your solution to assist the customer. It is very important when doing this to be aware of the body language accompanying your presentation; it is a great indicator to a "like or lost" scenario.

Customers pain tolerance could be introduced at this stage, suggesting that if the customer was not able to proceed to buying, what implications would arise.

AC—Always Be Closing

Listen to the customer's objections and don't rush into your answer. Think and respond to the objection, then watch the customer's response for agreement or disagreement. If you don't know the answers, say, "May I get back to you tomorrow with this answer," and make sure you do!

After answering objections successfully, point out, pull in the features and benefits of your product, and summarize them into a solution for the customer. At this stage, evaluate the customer's impression and look for buying signs or an agreement to consider, going forward. However, if at this stage you sense a nonbuying sign, ask if the solution is of assistance, and confirm the answer. You may at this stage need to go back to step 3 in the sales process.

Avoid Appearing Overly Pushy

Be confident in your position and offering. Draw the sale into a *win–win* situation, and do not be pushy.

Many Salespeople Fear the Closing Stage

Asking for the order is a precarious situation and, in some cases, you may feel you have got this in the bag, and the customer says no. "I will think about it"—they are being cautious and thorough. At this stage, if the customer has not said no, you are still in there. What do we do now? Asking the customer, "Have I covered all the product features adequately"? will at least provide you with a sense of acceptance.

What Is Most Important to the Customer during the Sales Process?

As a customer in buying mode, they are judging you constantly and also thinking of the following needs:

- Value for money, price, cost, competitiveness, customer service, and after-sales service. Keeping promises and reliability, maintaining quality, and ease of doing honest business. Meeting customer ego, customer aspirations and needs, service performance.
- Past performance as company reputation, and the company's readiness to help post point of sale.

Relationship Strategies

Here are a few of the tactics I advocate for building sales relationships and making the customer feel important:

- **Mutual interest:** People are drawn to those who are similar to themselves or have similar interests; if you can learn what mutual interest you share with the customer, be sure to engage them in conversation about it.

- **Ask for their opinions:** This shows not only that you value their insights, but that you can learn a lot from the prospect by encouraging them to share their knowledge and experience. Customers like to be asked questions and opinions.

- **Indicate that you care:** This is often achieved by demonstrating to the prospect that you'd like to remain informed. Ask about the customer's present situation and the outcomes he or she is seeking.

- **Compliments:** It's important to tell them not only what you like but why you like it; otherwise, you may be perceived as "insincere." The same is true of personal compliments. Be sure to focus on the individual's actions and not traits.

- **Past Rep!** If you are in the unfortunate position of filling in after a past rep who had a bad reputation and burnt many customers, my advice is to tread carefully and not to sell hard. Start by acknowledging the person's behavior and apologize, but say you are ethical and will not show such behavior yourself.

- **Be a challenger** (discussed in earlier chapters): The challenger is known for high sales achievement. What this means is challenging your customer for the best outcome for them.

- **Sales as a conversation:** In the end, the sales process must be seen as a natural and normal discussion. If it is disjointed, then the customer will be suspicious of lack of skills or of product knowledge.

Post-Sales Call Critique: A Critical Step in Self-Improvement

For many new salespeople, preparing the sales call and appointment, visiting the customer, and noting any follow-up required complete the call.

Unfortunately, it is not. Prior to walking to your car, sit for 5 minutes quietly and conduct a "post-sales call critique."

The reason for this is to look back on your SSO: the attention you received from your customer and whether you got through the seven sales steps and came out with a conclusion/close or moved forward with the opportunity. The critique is to enable you to be honest with yourself about the methods of selling you used and whether there are any areas of performance you can improve on.

The following questions are used as a guide: you can make up your own questions

- Were you on time for the appointment, and did you exchange business cards?
- Did you "gain favorable attention" from your customer, and were you relaxed?
- Did you understand the customer's position and needs, or did you stray from this?
- Did you find out who is the decision maker or makers/did you get their names?
- Did you find out when the customer needs to place their order (by what date)?
- Is the customer a KDM (key decision maker)?
- Did you center on the implications if the customer may not receive funding?
- In summing up, has the customer made a commitment to exploring further or ordering?
- Did the customer commit to seeing you again?
- Did you accomplish the SSO?

Helpful Hint

Again, review all these question in order. If you are getting a lot of "no" answers, look carefully at each question and assess why the answer is no. For instance, the customer shut down and did not give you the attention you needed. Why was this?

How to Self-Critique—Method Suggestion

If you are having problems with any of the items on the preceding check-list, ask your mentor or sales manager coach to visit customers with you and to watch your conduct over several sales calls. Rectifying bad habits is difficult. On recognizing the habit, work on one at a time, not an entire group of bad habits.

These Are More In-Depth Questions

- Did I sell correctly?
- Did I hold the customer's interest?
- Did I understand the customer's present needs?
- Did I emphasize the features and benefits?
- Did I simplify my presentation?
- Did I watch nonverbal signals?
- Did I answer the objections properly?
- Did I match the argument at the right time?

Critique Frequency

How many times a day should I critique myself? As you commence in sales and are still learning the skill, I would suggest that you critique yourself after every sale. Many salespeople come out of a sales call and say "I mucked up" and yet continue on without any positive change or self-reflection. You must identify where you need to improve.

Post-Sales Call Follow-Up Checklist

Sales is not the only task we do each day. There are a multitude of tasks we need to do each day to keep up. Here are some of them:

- **CRM/Sales** view entry of each sales call and information of the sale advance.
- **Project Sheet:** Call a meeting to advance the information and al-location of project tasks.

- **Tasks Entry:** Make notes of when the next sales call is to be, and enter appointment date.
- **Notes:** Enter into tasks what the customer needs quickly and follow-up dates to book.
- **Advance:** Consider what items you need, whom you need to engage, and when you need this engagement.
- You should write back to your customer, thanking them for their time and quoting the items you are forwarding on soon.

Post-Sales Data Entry

What Should I Put in My CRM/Sales View Notes So Others Fully Understand Too?

There are several types of CRM/Sales View entries. Some are too short and do not provide enough information, and some are much too long. I would suggest the following entry.

Date/day and customer that come up automatically on each entry.

Example 1: Sales call went well. Customer provided good time to establish position and department needs. Need centered on enough funding, and there are three decision makers—customer, John Johnson, and CEO Margret Smith. All others are low down on the KDM list. They need three new sheds constructed. Next step is *Quote requested.*

Example entry: could be shortened but does explain well for the viewer. It could be shortened a little or abbreviated into a sales code.

You have the order now—is this the end of my work? Congratulations!

Your first order has been sent through, and you are excited to prove yourself to your sales manager and team members. You receive some congratulatory calls, and you go home feeling quite chuffed. So you should. However, did you analyze why and how you succeeded?

The following questions may be of help

- Did you keep the customer's attention through the sales cycle?
- Did you offer a specific helpful customer solution?
- Did you engage other team members in the sale?

- Where could you improve even though you secured the sale?
- What can you do better?
- What did you do well to build on for future sales?

Securing your first sale feels wonderful, but this is only the beginning. Each subsequent sale will be different and require innovative selling techniques. "Selling is to me fun and exhilarating when it goes well, even on the worst of days; look for the good in each of your days activities." In addition, find the fun in dealing with different and various customer engagements.

When Do You Walk Away from a Sale and Why?

Walking away is difficult and hard. It's especially hard when you're walking away from a potential sale; after all, you've spent time, energy, and resources building a relationship, and giving up means you'll have nothing to show for it. But in the long run, knowing when to walk away and delete a lead will make you far more effective.[2]

The following reasons to cancel or delete an opportunity

1. **The prospect can't answer these three questions:** The sales process requires some detective skills. You need to gauge your prospect's pain threshold or pushing their bruise. This term is used to see if the customer will react to sensitive questions or problems that need solving.

   Ask yourself the following questions: What does success look like with this opportunity? Who else will be involved in this decision? By when do you need to have this opportunity completed?

   If the prospect says, "I don't know," it means that either he or she is not serious or is not a decision maker. And if it's the latter? Well, somewhere during the approval process, the real decision maker will ask her those same questions. Without a satisfactory response, the deal won't move forward. Just don't forget the customer is consulting the key decision makers up the line.

---

[2]W. Humphries. *3 Excellent Reasons You Should Walk Away from a Sale*, May 17, 2016. Three reasons to walk away, but there are many more than this example reference.

Before you give up, try saying, "I'm worried that unless we can figure out what you're hoping to accomplish—and by when—this might not be the best investment of your time. Should we take notes on our conversation and log this into CRM?"

2. **They really don't have the budget:** Salespeople are used to hearing "We don't have the budget" and "I can't afford that price." That shouldn't be your cue to give up; many prospects use price as a convenient excuse to get off the phone. However, some companies really won't be able to afford your product. Here's where you should try digging a little deeper.

3. **You're competing with three other vendors:** Given your line of work, you probably enjoy a little competition. Some sales managers are constantly reminded that "if we did go for this opportunity, we may have had a small chance of winning." But if you are competing with the preferred vendor, you need to know when to back off and move to another opportunity.

4. **They go quiet and dark, not taking your follow-up calls:** Out of nowhere, your prospect fell off the face of the cliff. They won't return your calls, answer your e-mails, or respond to your LinkedIn messages. Eventually, you turn to your sales manager to engage the customer. This scenario generally starts and continues for months until the customer announces the competitor has won the business.

5. **Working with a customer as a champion inside the account:** If a prospect is unable to introduce you to other stakeholders; talk about his or her budget; share their decision criteria; or answer your questions about their needs, desires, and pain points, he or she is likely a coach. This is someone who can be valuable in providing context around his or her company's internal politics and decision-making processes but lacks the authority or influence to impact a deal. Having a coach within the opportunity is a key role and can provide you with information about what is going on so you can adjust your target strategy actions. If the coach says, "Forget this deal, it won't happen," do you continue or abandon the prospect?

6. **They Don't See Your Value:** It's the salesperson's responsibility to educate the buyer on their solution's value. If your prospect is

struggling to understand why they need your product and how it will help achieve their goals, redefine your value proposition, show the customer case studies, send them testimonials from your happiest clients, and so on. The main thing is to identify the objection stopping the onward progress of the opportunity.

7. **It's Not a Good Fit:** If your product won't help the prospect, are you obligated to walk away? At the end of the day, your mission shouldn't be closing; it should be delivering the best solution to your customers.

    Imagine you are selling battery power tools to a mining company that is located miles from a generator. Think of the logic and if the customer would even see you at all.

Helpful Hint

To walk away from a sale is seen by many as committing suicide of sale ethics. Suggesting that you don't pursue every opportunity/lead is to some salespeople the worst of selling ethics.

I, on the other hand, think it is smart business to walk away if the work up of the opportunity has been exhaustively thrashed out, and all key stakeholders agree too, then move onto the next opportunity.

Walking away from an opportunity should be a collaborative decision, no jut the sales manager. You as the sales person will play a big role on this final decision.

CHAPTER 13

How to Ultimately Tell the Buying Signs of Your Customer

There is a plethora of information on the web discussing and analyzing customer buyer behavior. We have touched on buyer behavior and its psychology, but to me it is the most important process to master and understand.

Coming out of sales and coaching, I wish I could master this process without the mystique that surrounds it. Many professional salespeople I know say, "I use my gut feeling in the end" to ascertain the customer buying position, meaning, "I look at the responses and body language of my customer and make up my mind on that alone." Unfortunately, I and many others have been wrong at times.

I would say about 95 percent of salespeople entering into a key sale with multiple KDMs involved need to know where they sit in the sales cycle, who is on your side, and whom you need to work on further. Again, emphasizing the use of project sheets to identify who is a KDM and to identify the true buyers is a good starting point. Even the most experienced salesperson is still perplexed, with some customers' decision-making processes. The following is a list to consider:

These are some of the buying and non-buying behaviors to look out for:
- The customer who will not give away his or her thoughts and decision.
- The buyer who gives you continual feedback but will not give you any indication.
- The customer who likes you but is not saying too much about his or her decision.

- The buyer who is always on your side (a coach) and guides you in the right direction.
- The customer who likes your solution but dislikes being with you (personal dislike issues).
- The customer who will buy from you always, regardless.
- Some of the preceding behaviors are, under certain circumstances, mixed together and confuse the seller further.
- The customer who continually sends you up the wrong path.

My strategy is not to let buying signs or behavior influence me until we have established relationships and product fit to customer need, and priced acceptability is understood.

Some say the order is not in until the f...t lady sings.

Using body language assessment is important with the checklist of customer behavioral traits. Let's look at a few:

Posture is a key to the openness of the customer and their seating positions. The customer gaze shows interest or disinterest in your message; the face and expression are key as you engage directly with people. The customer is easily distracted and will answer their phone, disregarding your presence, even avoiding eye contact.

The Negative Body Language to Look Out for

The customer has crossed their arms, showing disapproval and lack of genuine interest in your solution. If the customer leans away and you lose the body–eye connection, again, disinterest is the overall message. If the customer refuses to look you in the eye and has no genuine eye contact, you have lost GFA (gaining favorable attention), or the customer has more important things to do and you are wasting their time.

If the customer can't remove themselves from the e-mail or phone and places objects on the table in your view, this is a distracting practice. If he or she shows a great deal of fidgeting, tapping, distractedness, or a

Note: After numerous approaches to the Miller Heiman corporation and their new owner, to seek their approval to mention certain products such as Blue Sheets or SPIN, they refused to reply to all our approaches we made.

complete lack of interest in your presence in the room, you have to start again. Finally, if the customer makes excuses to end the meeting prematurely ("sorry, Mark, I have to go now"), I would review your initial approach.

All these negative body movements and posturing send a clear sign of disinterest and lack of positive body language. To come back from this point is difficult, but I would recommend the following solution.

In most cases, if you have lost your customer's attention, pushing the reset button is necessary; but how do you do this? The salesperson has to think quickly and ask a pertinent question—"Jan I feel I have not proposed the right solution for your company needs."

This is why you need to know the 7 steps of the sale process.

Poor past representation takes time to repair, and your customer is constantly critiquing every move you make and request they ask for. It is vital in this situation that you do all requested tasks on time and professionally so as to regain faith and trust. Regaining trust takes a great deal of time to secure, so be patient, methodical, respectful of the customer, and, under no circumstances, talk over them; the customer must feel they are in charge.

Positive Body Language (But Watch Out)

We would all like to encounter positive body language at every sale; however, this is not the real world. Even the most positive reaction from your customer does not assure the sale. Essentially, you want to see the following body and eye language reactions: friendly facial expressions, positive body posture, direct eye contact, customer touch such as a firm handshake, customer voice modulation, which may be loud, medium, or soft. Pay attention to inconsistencies but will be forgiving of your silly mistakes, and the customer will laugh with you in the conversation—a general friendliness.

These are some of the tell-tale signs that may ensure you are on the right track for good communication skills while moving through the sale.

However, even if you receive positive body language and you think you are "in," the customer could be just a friendly person but not showing buying signs.

Here Are Some Tips to Help Your Own Body Language—Be Mindful of Your Presentation

- Prep with an open and conducive pose when seated, not too powerful.
- Fire up your energy level so you are ready to sell.
- Always smile and look attentive for your customer.
- Don't pretend you know everything.
- Don't gesture above your shoulders, and keep your hands and arms to your side or on your lap.
- Use your hands when talking, but do not overdo this.
- Use props to engage such as a tablet or a brochure.
- Be totally respectful to your customer.
- Do not overdress according to the industry you are selling in.
- When jotting down notes, try to keep your eye contact as best you can.
- Avoid the pauses that sometimes enter the sales.
- Keep calm and be the listener, not the major talker.

Summary: Are Female Salespeople Better Than Male Sellers?

My personal opinion is that women are way more perceptive than the majority of male sellers. Women appear to be able to spot incongruence between the spoken word and body language during the personal sales contact.[1]

This is especially in a female to female sales situation.

Psychologists at Harvard University conducted a study that showed that women pay more attention to body language than men. Why is this? The participants were asked to watch a short video of a conversation between a man and a woman. The participants were asked to decide what was going on by reading their expressions. The women scored accurately 87 percent, and men 42 percent.

So, on the basis of research and anecdotal evidence of men versus women sellers, the women should be selling more and being more

---

[1]Science of https://www.scienceofpeople.com/gender-differences/.

successful. My hunch is that male versus female success rates in general sales are equal across the board but that female sellers get past this stage faster.[2]

The further question which should be explored is: are male sellers better to male customers? My hunch in this case is that the conversation will take on a more blocky discussion. This does not determine the sales end result.

Either way, it is the fit for the position that determines the end result.

Selling in Summary

When I first began in sales, I thought this would take a long time to master. Well, sorry, it takes a lifetime to master. As we grow, we are able to learn more complex lessons and tasks.

Corporate training in product and sales should take priority, and ongoing field coaching should be a part of company policy whether the company has a trainer or coach or not; if not; the sales manager should assume this role. Unfortunately, the research is tragic for this ongoing problem, and I hope this book has highlighted the need for effective training.

Conclusion

In the end, your company will forget you quickly (Jim who?) and move on with your replacement. If you think you are irreplaceable, then think again. Big global sales organizations care little about you in the end. You are just a number to achieve the overall sales budget. Yes, they do care about people but if you are not performing to their expectations, you will have a limited tenure. This has become the DNA of selling for global organisations.

Setting aside the personal contacts you develop within your team, higher up the food chain, your worth to the senior management team, working in a faraway country, means little. So an understanding of your

---

[2]Who's Better at Selling: Men or Women? Data from 30,469 Sales Calls/Written by Chris Orlob/Current research seems to place women with the upper hand in sales today.

Me Brand and the skill you bring to the table is what you provide to your company. Your worth is valuable to companies while you are performing, but when times are lean in sales, management will move you on very quickly.

In the end your Me brand Is the promise of another job in another company that may appreciate your skills. Keep honing this talent and protect it with a great deal of vigor.

I find it sad that we, as a sales profession, have been accepting of such poor corporate behavior. We can only blame ourselves for allowing such disgraceful business behavior to proliferate; if we had been willing to push back against this behavior in the 1960s, I am sure our position would be more valued now.

Australian Qualitative Research

It was a surprise to me that the research results came in with such a low score. This confirmed to me that there was a need to uncover the truth. One particular company I researched early on was so low in its score, I was really surprised. I interviewed sales managers apart from salespeople, and, unfortunately, they colored their answers with mistruths, trying to pump up their position to cover up what was really going on. There were a few sales managers that held high positions and told the truth about the treatment of sales professionals.

A review of the overall results shows an average of 40 companies rated job satisfaction at 53 percent, indicating that *47 percent* of salespeople are having problems and that their company is not addressing their needs. Yes, you can pick the eyes out of this research, but the numbers don't lie, especially as low as they are.

The purpose of this book is to bring to the attention of salespeople the pitfalls of working for global organizations and reveal that the way business is run is at the expense of salespeople satisfaction. I don't bear a grudge against these organizations; however, I want them to understand that salespeople are the key to their success and hence that the overall training and support are necessary.

Being happy in our job is the final clue to a successful career in selling. Being healthy and having the support of your organization are the priorities; everything then falls into place. I do hope that whoever reads this book takes stock of his or her own organization's performance and endeavors to improve the life and careers of professional salespeople.

If I have perhaps given some simple but profound help to you, I have been successful too.

Overall Australian Research Results

To be completed by		Researcher—Eden D. White		
Deadline:		January 1, 2016 to June 25, 2018 to be completed by June 25, 2018		
Percentage	Planning & Prep phase.	De By	Outcome Notes	
100	Planning timelines	January 1, 2016	all planning to be completed by due date	
100	Preparation of timelines	January 1, 2017	all preparation also to be completed by due date, with all 78 questions of research completed	
100	To interview 40 candidates; to be completed by December 1, 2017	December 25, 2017	ensure all candidates' data entry completed by due dates	
100	Enter data and compile by December 15, 2017	December 25, 2017	compile data and report on overall results of 10 elements recorded	
	Research 10 Element Questions (rating of 1 to 10) for each question		Notes recorded	
65	1. Sales Force: Describe your overall satisfaction with your current sales position	December 25, 2017	35% of respondents were dissatisfied with their job satisfaction	
71	2. Relationships: What importance does the company place on their sales professionals?	December 25, 2017	71% thought they did OK, but 29% were scathing about the lack of overall support.	
61	3. Management: What importance does management place on company sales staff?	December 25, 2017	39% of sales staff considered their management did little to keep good performers.	
65	4. Recruiting: Do you think recruitment agencies provide all the appropriate assistance?	December 25, 2017	35% of respondents were very unhappy with the ethics and assistance from recruiters.	

(continued)

To be completed by		Researcher—Eden D. White	
63	5. **Training & CRM:** Could your company do better in product & sales training?	December 25, 2017	37% of respondents said their companies were below par for training programs. Although 63% of respondents claimed their company was making an effort, they reported that they trained in product well but not in selling the product effectively.
61	6. **Personal:** Do you believe companies provide appropriate support for sales professionals?	December 25, 2017	61% said they did, but 31% said their companies performed very poorly in this regard
76	7. **Incentives & Salary:** Do you think incentive schemes provide drive to work harder?	December 25, 2017	24% of respondents said incentive schemes did not drive them to work harder; however, 76% said they did; many commented on the complicated mathematics in their commission schemes and the timing for payment & honesty. In addition, many said their commission paid was the last thought on their mind but liked the idea of being paid extra for effort and achievement above budget.
59	8. **Performance:** What effort does your company make to keep good salespeople?	December 25, 2017	41% said their companies were genuinely motivated to keep good sales staff, but 29% said they did not care about keeping good sales staff.
35	9. **Occupation Health & Safety** Do you think your company takes all precautions to ensure the safety & welfare of all sales staff?	December 25, 2017	65% of sales staff interviewed expressed concern over their companies' attitude regarding their welfare and safety. This is the highest negative score recorded for the research.

To be completed by		Researcher—Eden D. White	
41	10. **General:** Does your company provide all the tools salespeople need to be successful?	December 25, 2017	Another sad response from 59% of respondents, saying they do not receive the sales tool support they need to be successful salespersons.

Key Research Feedback Results			
51%	Overall wellness and satisfactory score	December 25, 2017	Of all 40 interviewed candidates, the overall wellness and satisfaction average of their organization performance was reported to be very low, at 51%. Many respondents had severe unhappiness and complained their companies did not support them in many key areas. Specific issues centered on lying and deception before and during the employment stage, commission issues, lack of training for product knowledge, and lack of in-field training on how to sell the product. Lack of leadership was also cited as a critical problem with sales managers and the loss of ongoing support as a new salesperson. Job satisfaction was important and consistent through the survey. The lack of product and sales training and a general lack of support contributed largely to the low satisfaction score. HR recorded a low score, citing lack of support during sales team conflict and the inability to resolve it. In addition, companies paying lip service to safety and working late night hours remained constant in the research.
54%	Overall score for all data average score		54 out of 100 points was the average score.
23%	Female interviewees #		23% were female.
67%	Male interviewees #		67% were male.
92%	Number of medical/device/capital survey interviews		92% of medical/device and capital people interviewed.

(*continued*)

Key Research Feedback Results			
57%	Number of over-all salespeople interviewed		6% overall of trainers interviewed.
27%	Number of sales managers interviewed		
26%	Others interviewed		In the candidate list, only 10% were female.

Reference Listing

The listed references are suggested for good reading

Reference List	Topic
001	Quotation from Thomas Edison
002	The 80/20 Rule of Sales: How to Find Your Best Customers
003	Researcher, E. White 2016/2017 over 40 global companies' results
004	Psychosocial work environment and mental health among traveling salespeople/Article: October 26, 2010
005	Field Coaching Best Practices for Sales Managers—Published on June 28, 2014
006	Striking a balance between proactive and in-the-field sales coaching
007	New Scientist, January 27, 2018, studying workplace stress/Denmark
008	Information overload in sales—a recent study, by marketing research firm CSO Insights,
009	Trait test for reader, Eden White, 2017
010	Work Ombudsman, http://www.fairwork.gov.au/resources/best-practice-guides/Pages/a-guide-for-young-workers.asp
011	Are Sales Teams Bullying CPG Senior Management to Reject Change? By CPGToolBox, Jun 29, 2016, Blog
012	March 25, 2011March 25, 2011—Managing A Prima Donna Salesperson
013	Corporate deception: where do we draw the line on lying at work? July 1, 2016, 9.35 pm AEST
014	What to do when your Boss Lies: How to Take Action—Chitra Reddy
015	How to deal With Stress in Sales, Published November 23, 2016 by Nick Hedges. Nick Hedges discusses the same issues we have dealt with, stress being the precursor to burnout.
016	G. Harris, G. Mayho, and L. Page. 2003. "Occupational Health Issues Affecting the Pharmaceutical Sales Force." *Occupational Medicine* 53:378–383. doi:10.1093/occmed/kqg118

Reference List	Topic
017	Article EE Roughed, 1 August 1999, APMA Code of conduct. G. Harris, G. Mayho, and L. Page. 2003. "Occupational Health Issues Affecting the Pharmaceutical Sales Force." *Occupational Medicine* 53:378–383. doi:10.1093/occmed/kqg118.
018	2 personal accounts of mistrust from an employer
019	Differences Between B2C & B2B in Business Systems/by Ian Linton; reviewed by Michelle Seidel, B.Sc., LL.B., MBA; Updated January 29, 2019
020	Executives' perspectives of the changing role of the sales profession: views from France, the United States, and Mexico. The customer relationship management (CRM) market will be worth $37 billion in 2017.
021	Posted by Stacy Bouchard, August 26, 2015 1:00:00 PM
022	Provo study, December 2016
023	Sales Commission Structures: Which Model is Best for Reps?
024	The Disadvantages of Percentage-Based Sales Commission Plans/ Author Luke Author
025	Are these commission issues causing you to lose reps, Kendra Lee, October 2014
026	Sales Budget: Definition & Examples—by S. Robert, February 14, 2018
027	Sales Territory Alignment: An Overlooked...—Semantic Scholar
028	Medicines Australia's Code of Conduct, which was established in 1960, has been revised on a regular basis. Code of Conduct Edition 18
029	UK—The ABPI Code of Practice for the Pharmaceutical Industry 2018
030	Health Care Division Bureau of Competition Federal Trade Commission Washington DC 20580 and FDA 2018
031	the current state of sales training US
039	7 Reasons Why Sales Training Fails
032	The poison that's killing your sales, July 5, 2017, John Bedwany. B2B, Sales, Social Selling B2B, Strategic Selling
033	Lack of Corporate Training as #1 Driver of the "Skills Gap" September 2015
034	Preparing New Sales Reps for Success: The Importance of On-the-Job Training and Coaching, May 1, 2017, Taryn Oesch, CPTM
035	Posted by Carole Mahoney/the science of role play to improve sales.
036	CSO Insights 2016 Sales Enablement Optimization Study

(continued)

Reference List	Topic
037	Ashok Sharma, May 10, 2017, Corporate learning 5 Key Strategies to Improve Sales Training and Development Within Your organization
038	5 Types of Selling Styles—Which One is Yours?
039	Selling Styles for Successful Salespeople. Posted on June 20, 2008 in Selling Skills
040	How to Adopt a Sales Mindset—Thirteen simple rules to become your own sales superstar
041	9 Bad Sales Habits Every Rep Should Avoid—James Meincke, January 3, 2019
042	Procrastinating: how to stop it so you can sell more, by Anis 2018
043	Maslow's hierarchy of needs
044	The benefits of mentoring new salepersons by Ray Taylor, April 29, 2016
045	Sales Courses/find your right fit online first
046	Identifying the 5 Key Decision Makers in the Sales Process, October 2018 by Zachary Cohen
047	Pipeline research by Wendy Connick, October 2017
048	What is a Sales Funnel, Examples and How to Create One (Guide) Home Analytics Last Updated on January 15, 2019
049	Blue Sheets—Not Just for the "Sales" Department, December 2, 2017
050	How to Overcome Fear of Selling, May 30, 2012 by Susan Martin
051	4 Things Mentally Strong Salespeople Do That Average Reps Don't
052	Nine ways to overcome fear of rejection in sales
053	Prospecting the future.
054	200+ Sales Statistics You Must Know—Real Data for 2019 & Beyond
055	The Harvard Business Review/cold call issues
056	Teaching Sales/Suzanne Fogel, David Hoffmeister, Richard Rocco, Daniel P. Strunk, *Harvard Business Review*
057	3 Excellent Reasons You Should Walk Away from a Sale. May 17, 2016, Will Humphries
058	Science of https://www.scienceofpeople.com/gender-differences/
059	Who's Better at Selling: Men or Women? Data From 30,469 Sales Calls/Written by Chris Orlob
060	Inbound organization – How to build and strengthen your company's future using inbound principles by t Hockenberry 2018.

Source: Hubspot consumer behavior survey, (2016) 43% of consumers want more video content in 2017.

Please note: after numerous approaches to the Miller Heiman corporation and their new owner, to seek their approval to mention certain products such as Blue Sheets or SPIN, the refused to reply to all our approaches we made.

Glossary

The following terms are generally used in sales and could help you understand the sales industry further. Please note, these terms will vary from country to country. Sales and marketing teams are both responsible for the growth and revenue side of the business and yet sometimes talk a different language.

1. **ABC:** Always be closing.
2. **AIDA:** Attention, interest, desire, action.
3. **Benefit:** The value of a product or service that a consumer of that product or service experiences. Benefits are distinct from features, and sales reps should sell based on benefits that are *supported* by features.
4. **BANT:** Budget, authority, need, timeline.

   B = Budget: Determines whether your prospect has a budget for what you're selling.

   A = Authority: Determines whether your prospect has the authority to make a purchasing decision.

   N = Need: Determines whether there's a business need for what you're selling.

   T = Timeline: Determines the time frame for implementation.

5. **Bullying:** being unduly harassed and pressured unnecessarily in sales.
6. **Bottom of the funnel** (BOFU) A stage of the buying process leads reach when they're just about to close into new customers. They've identified a problem, have shopped around for possible solutions, and are very close to buying.

   6a Buying process/cycle: The process potential buyers go through before deciding whether to make a purchase. Although it's been broken down into many substages to align with different business models, it can universally be boiled down to these three life cycle stages.

7. **Always be closing:** An antiquated sales strategy that basically says everything a sales rep does throughout the sales process is in pursuit of the singular goal of closing a deal.

8. **Buying signal:** A communication from a prospect indicating they are ready to make a purchase, either verbal or nonverbal.

9. **Closed opportunities:** An umbrella term that includes both closed-won and closed-lost opportunities, although some people use it to mean only closed-won opportunities.

    9a. Closed-won: When a sales rep closes a deal in which the buyer purchases the product or service.

    9b. Closed-lost: When a sales rep closes a deal in which the buyer does not purchase the product or service.

    9c. Closing ratio: The percentage of prospects that a sales rep successfully close-wins. This ratio is usually used to assess individual sales reps on their short-term performance.

    9d. Commission: The payment a sales rep gets when they successfully sell a product or service.

10. **CRM—customer relations management (tool):** Software that lets companies keep track of everything they do with their existing and potential customers. At the simplest level, CRM software lets you keep track of all the contact information for these customers.

11. **Cold calling**: Making unsolicited calls in an attempt to sell products or services. It's also a very inefficient way to find potential customers.

12. **Consumer:** A person who uses a product or service. They may not be the actual buyer of that product; for example, if I buy my brother a pair shoes, then my brother is the consumer of those shoes, not me.

13. **Competitor:** A person or company that you are in sales competitive selling.

14. **Cross-selling:** When a sales rep has more than one type of product to offer consumers that could be beneficial and he or she successfully sells a consumer more than one item either at the time of purchase or later on.

15. **Forecasting:** Estimating future sales performance for a forecast period based on historical data. Forecasted performance can vary widely from actual sales results but helps sales reps plan their upcoming days, weeks, and months and helps high-level employees set standards for expenses, profit, and growth.

    G = Goals: Determine the quantifiable goals your prospect wants or needs to hit. An opportunity for sales reps to establish themselves as an advisor by beginning to help prospects reset or quantify their goals.

P = **Plans**: Determine the prospect's current plans that they'll implement in order to achieve those goals.

C = **Challenges**: Determine whether the sales rep can help a prospect overcome their and their company's challenges; ones they're dealing with and ones they (or the sales rep) anticipate.

T = **Timeline**: Determines the time frame for implementation of their goals and plans and when they need to eliminate their challenges.

B = **Budget**: Determines how much money a prospect has to spend.

A = **Authority**: Determines who in the organization will help champion and/or decide to make a purchase.

C = **Negative consequences**: Discuss the negative things that'll happen if a prospect doesn't meet their goal.

I = **Positive implications**: Discuss the positive outcomes that'll happen if a prospect meets their goal.

16. **KDM—Key decision maker**: The person who, or role that, makes the final decision of a sale; they are often "guarded" by a gatekeeper.

17. **Lead qualification:** The process of determining whether a potential buyer has certain characteristics that qualify him or her as a lead. These characteristics could be budget, authority, timeline, and so on.

18. **Loss leader:** Used in retail to refer to a product sold at a low price (either at breakeven or at a loss) for the purpose of attracting customers into the store. The goal is for customers who go into the store to buy other items that are priced to make a profit.

19. **Margin:** The difference between a product or service's selling price and the cost of production.

20. **The funnel:** The stage that a lead enters after identifying a problem. Now, they're looking to conduct further research to find a solution to the problem. The stage is an entry into CRM.

21. **Top of the funnel:** The very first stage of the buying process. Leads at this stage are identifying a problem they have and are looking for more information. At this point, marketers create helpful content that aids lead in identifying this problem and providing next steps toward a solution.

22. **Pipeline:** The step-by-step process sales reps go through to convert a prospect into a customer. The sales pipeline is often divided into stages for each step in the sales process, and the sales rep is responsible for moving opportunities through the stages.

23. **Pipeline weighted:** A more detailed version of a sales pipeline, in which each opportunity is given a specific value based on which stage they're at in the sales process.

24. **Prospect sales call:** The first call a sales rep makes to a prospect. Prospecting, the process of searching for and finding potential buyers. Sales reps (or "prospectors") seek out qualified prospects and move them through the sales cycle.

    A—Objection: A prospect's challenge to or rejection of a product or service's benefits and a natural part of the sales process. Common objections often have to do with budget, authority, need, and timing (see BANT). How sales reps handle objections plays a big role in determining whether a prospect will buy. Learn how to tackle common B2B sales objections here.

    B—Opportunity: Although every company has different processes for defining what criteria make someone an opportunity, it's basically when a qualified lead is being worked by Sales. See Qualified Lead for more information.

    C—Pain point: A prospect's pain point, or need, is the most important thing for a sales rep to identify in the selling process. Without knowing a prospect's pain points, they can't possibly offer benefits to help resolve those pain points.

    D—Performance plan: Also "Performance Improvement Plan" or "PIP." A sales rep is put on a performance plan if he or she doesn't make a certain percentage of quota over a certain period of time. Performance plans vary from company to company, but they usually start with a written warning and further disciplinary action, including termination, if necessary. The purpose of performance plans is to set clear and specific performance goals, provide a means for feedback, and develop sales skills.

    E—Positioning statement: Statements and questions that sales reps use when opening a sales call to engage the prospect in conversation around their *pain points.*

25. **Quota:** A sales goal; a set amount of selling a sales rep is expect to meet over a given time frame, usually a month and/or a quarter. It's very, very common for sales reps to have quotas; also, the form they take can vary from company to company and from role to role.

26. **Qualified lead:** A contact that opted in to receive communication from your company, became educated about your product or service, and is interested in learning more. Marketing and Sales often have two different versions of qualified leads (MQLs for Marketing and SQLs for Sales), so be sure to have conversations with your sales team to set expectations for the types of leads you plan to hand over.

27. **Selling:** A meeting between a seller and a buyer to discuss a proposition.

28. **Upselling:** when a sales rep sells an existing customer a higher-end version of the product that the customer originally bought.

29. **Value proposition:** A benefit of a product or company intended to make it more attractive to potential buyers and differentiate it from competitors.

30. **Slang terms you should know:**
    - **Talk the talk:** get the results.
      Get the business, achieve sales.
    - **Bluebird:** guaranteed to put you in a cheerful mood, a bluebird is a lucrative sales opportunity that drops into your lap.
    - **In the bag:** a sale that is said to be about to happen.
    - **Go live:** the product is in use.
    - **Going to trial:** the customer is trying before buying.
    - **Buying signals:** the customer is showing buying signs.
    - **Closed question:** a closed question is typically a yes-or-no question that directs a prospect toward making a choice or taking a position.
    - **Open question:** the opposite of the preceding term.
    - **Emotional sale:** using the customer's emotions to draw the sale in.

Other Terms Used in Sales

1. **Active buyers:** Buyers who are active in a buying journey and looking for solutions.

2. **Account executive:** Sales team members that close deals with sales-qualified opportunities.

3. **Attention, interest, desire, action (AIDA):** A method of motivating people to buy by gaining their attention, interest, and desire for the product and then inspiring them to take action.

4. **Account manager:** A sales role responsible for managing a large customer account or group of large accounts.

5. **Awareness stage:** The first stage of the buyer's journey. A buyer who is at the awareness stage will have realized and expressed symptoms of a potential problem but will not yet know how to solve it.

6. **Before–after bridge (BAB):** Cold e-mail formula. Open by describing a problem that is relevant to your prospect and then describe how the world would be different if that problem didn't exist.

7. **Bounce rate (BR):** The percentage of e-mail addresses that didn't receive the message you sent because the message was returned by the mail server or client.

8. **Buyer persona:** A representation of your ideal customer that describes who they are, what their objectives are, what motivates them, how they think, and where and when they buy.

9. **Customer acquisition cost (CAC):** It is calculated by simply dividing all the costs incurred on acquiring more customers (marketing expenses) by the number of customers acquired in the period the money was spent.

10. **Customer churn rate:** A metric used to measure customer retention and value. CR = (number of customers at beginning of measurement period – number of customers at end of measurement period)/ (number of customers at beginning of measurement period).

11. **Customer lifetime value (CLV):** A prediction that connects net profit to the entire future relationship of a customer.

12. **Click through rate (CTR):** The percentage of people who clicked through, for example, on a link in an e-mail. For online ads, it is measured as the number of unique clicks divided by the number of times that an ad is shown (impressions).

13. **Conversion form:** Also known as lead capture form, it is typically found on a landing page and collects details about visitors, usually in exchange for a content offer. When visitors complete a form for

the first time, their information is added to your database, making them a lead.

14. **Conversion path:** This is the lead capture journey site visitors go through. In a typical process, a visitor will first click a CTA that leads to a landing page and complete a conversion form (which redirects to a thank you page containing a content offer), causing them to convert to a lead.

15. **Conversion rate:** The number of people who take an action divided by the number of people who could have.

16. **Cross-selling:** The process of identifying current customers, determining the product or services that they aren't using, and encouraging them to buy based on their need and a preexisting satisfaction with the company.

17. **Call-to-action (CTA):** A sentence or phrase that tells people what to do, for example, "Schedule a call," "Click here," "Buy now."

18. **Customer experience (CX):** All the interactions a customer has with your business and could involve usage of your product, engaging with your website, communicating with your sales team, and so on.

19. **Customer journey:** The customer journey spans a variety of touchpoints by which the customer moves from awareness to engagement and purchase. Successful brands focus on developing a seamless experience that ensures each touchpoint interconnects and contributes to the overall journey.

20. **E-mail workflow:** A series of e-mails triggered when a lead enters your database. Typically starting with a thank you e-mail and access to a content offer, workflow e-mails are used to nurture leads and build a relationship through the funnel.

21. **E-mail service provider (ESP):** A company that helps senders create and deliver e-mail campaigns.

22. **Emotional sale:** A selling method that attempts to appeal to a buyer's emotions by either generating desire and excitement around the product's benefits or evoking negative emotions like fear and frustration: pain points that your product or service can alleviate.

23. **Features, advantages, benefits (FAB):** An acronym used to remind salespeople to focus on the benefits a customer will gain from the product rather than on what they're selling.

24. **Intellectual sale:** This attempts to appeal to a prospect's logic and their need for a quick, affordable solution to a problem. An intellectual sale is more "business" than "personal."

25. **Marketing qualified lead (MQL):** A lead that has demonstrated some level of interest in your product/service and fits criteria determined by the marketing team that indicates it is more likely to become a customer as compared with other leads.

26. **Marketing qualification representative (MQR):** Inside sales reps tasked with following up with leads that have engaged with marketing content.

27. **Month-to-date (MTD):** A period starting at the beginning of the current month and ending at the current date.

28. **Reply rate:** A measurement of a number of people who respond to an e-mail. You can improve this by *personalizing your e-mails.*

29. **Request for proposal:** An invitation issued by a company to solicit vendor bids for products, solutions, or services.

30. **Return on investment (ROI):** What you get back from an investment of money, time, or talent.

31. **Software as a service (SaaS):** Businesses that offer services via software available online or downloaded to your computer.

32. **Sales enablement:** Providing inbound sales executives with the marketing insight and business intelligence (BI) they need to advise buyers at the right moment and build trusted relationships.

33. **Sales triggers:** An event that creates an opening for a sales opportunity; for example, a company announcing that it's expanding to a new location could present an upsell or introduction opportunity.

34. **Sandbagging:** Holding off on closing active deals once you've already hit your quota/commission for the month so that you can more easily hit your numbers the following month.

35. **Side selling:** Selling a complementary product or service to a prospect who is using a competitor for your main product.

36. **Smile and dial:** Cold calling with a cheerful, positive tone of voice: a smile. Smiling communicates warmth and trustworthiness over the phone, making the prospect less likely to hang up on you. Even if people can't see your smile, they can hear it.

37. **Sales-qualified lead (SQL):** An SQL is the sales team affirming that it's a good lead with a potential opportunity.

About the Author

Eden White is a married Australian resident, with three adult children and four grandchildren. My family live in Australia, except my youngest son, who lives in Lund, Sweden, completing his PhD.

My working career has spanned over 49 years in the medical device and capital industry, incorporating professional sales, sales management, management coaching, and 13 years running my own medical distributorship in Melbourne, Australia. During this time in the medical industry, I have spent over 25 years as a professional sales coach and mentor. In addition, I spent 11 years as a business and sales manager for two companies, working throughout the Asia Pacific region.

Over my 49-year career in sales and sales management, I have been honored with over 10 national sales awards, several world marketing awards, and many "best in sales" awards for achievement. I have qualifications in operating room technique, wound closure, and specific urology awards. I also hold several management awards and a Cert 4 in T&A 4010 for coaching and assessment.

I retired from the industry 4 years ago to begin writing my manuscript; however, the research did take longer than anticipated—over 14 months. At the end of the research, it became obvious that there were problems and concerns within the professional sales industry, with over 50 percent of research interviewees unhappy in their current positions. I documented and tabulated the findings from this research, which has formed a huge part of my book. I was surprised to find the overseas research similar and therefore resolved to help salespeople in general with a go-to resource such as this.

Currently, I am writing my second book (sales management, a license to manage), aimed at sales managers, and a third will follow for sales coaches.

Index

OTHER TITLES IN BUSINESS
CAREER DEVELOPMENT COLLECTION

Vilma Barr, *Editor*

- *Financing New Ventures: An Entrepreneur's Guide to Business Angel Investment* by Geoffrey Gregson
- *Strategic Bootstrapping* by Matthew W. Rutherford
- *Be Different!: The Key to Business and Career Success* by Stanley W. Silverman
- *Introduction to Business: A Primer On Basic Business Operations* by Patrice Flynn
- *Present! Connect!: A Guide to Creating and Delivering Presentations That Capture, Entertain, and Connect to Any Audience* by Tom Guggino

Announcing the Business Expert Press Digital Library

Concise e-books business students need for classroom and research

This book can also be purchased in an e-book collection by your library as

- a one-time purchase,
- that is owned forever,
- allows for simultaneous readers,
- has no restrictions on printing, and
- can be downloaded as PDFs from within the library community.

Our digital library collections are a great solution to beat the rising cost of textbooks. E-books can be loaded into their course management systems or onto students' e-book readers.

The **Business Expert Press** digital libraries are very affordable, with no obligation to buy in future years. For more information, please visit **www.businessexpertpress.com/librarians**. To set up a trial in the United States, please email **sales@businessexpertpress.com**.

www.ingramcontent.com/pod-product-compliance
Lightning Source LLC
Chambersburg PA
CBHW061159220326
41599CB00025B/4539